D1356588

Please return/renew this item by the last date shown on this label, or on your self-service receipt.

To renew this item, visit **www.librarieswest.org.uk** or contact your library

Your borrower number and PIN are required.

4 5 0021781 4

THE LANDMARK LIBRARY

Chapters in the History of Civilization

The Landmark Library is a record of the achievements of humankind from the late Stone Age to the present day. Each volume in the series is devoted to a crucial theme in the history of civilization, and offers a concise and authoritative text accompanied by a generous complement of images. Contributing authors to The Landmark Library are chosen for their ability to combine scholarship with a flair for communicating their specialist knowledge to a wider, non-specialist readership.

THE RITE OF SPRING

GILLIAN MOORE

HEAD
of ZEUS

An Apollo Book

For my family

This is an Apollo book, first published
in the UK in 2019 by Head of Zeus Ltd

1 3 5 7 9 10 8 6 4 2

A CIP catalogue record for this book is
available from the British Library.

ISBN (HB) 9781786696823
ISBN (HB) 9781786696816

Designed by Isambard Thomas
Printed in Spain by Graficas Estella

Head of Zeus Ltd
First Floor East
5–8 Hardwick Street
London EC1R 4RG

WWW.HEADOFZEUS.COM

Introduction

Afavourite anecdote about Igor Stravinsky concerns a dinner in honour of his eightieth birthday hosted by President and Mrs Kennedy at the White House on 18 June 1962. The evening was a rather awkward, formal affair. Most of the guests had little knowledge of Stravinsky's music, although a few of his friends had been invited to make him feel more relaxed. The composer-conductor Leonard Bernstein was there, as was the composer Nicolas Nabokov and Stravinsky's record producer Goddard Lieberson. The event was taking place at the height of the Cold War and Stravinsky was under no illusion about the political agenda behind his invitation. The administration knew that he was planning to visit his native Russia later that year, for the first time since 1914. War and revolution had kept him away for nearly five decades. His adopted homeland wanted to pre-empt the Soviet Union and claim him as its own. At the White House dinner, Stravinsky took full advantage of the freely flowing alcohol to lubricate the social wheels and he clearly warmed to the Kennedys themselves. At the end of the evening, as the rather drunk composer was waved off in his car by the presidential couple, he turned to his wife Vera and said, 'Nice kids.'[1]

It takes self-confidence to refer to the president of the United States and the first lady as 'nice kids'. But Stravinsky had earned it. He lived between 1882 and 1971. Along with a small handful of cultural figures – luminaries who distinguished themselves in other artistic areas, including his near contemporaries Pablo Picasso, Charlie Chaplin, Coco Chanel, Alfred Hitchcock and Louis Armstrong – he was one of the individuals who helped define culture in what might be termed the thick end of the twentieth century. He became famous just as the century began. The course of his long life was deeply affected by its major conflicts and political convulsions. Thanks to twentieth-century technology his music spread across the globe. Stravinsky had an enormous influence on the soundtrack of the century, not just in

Vera Stravinsky, John F. Kennedy, Jackie Kennedy and Igor Stravinsky
in Washington, 1962.

its classical concert halls but in its cinemas, rock venues and jazz clubs. His musical kleptomania – he is, after all, one of several people to whom the aphorism 'lesser artists borrow; great artists steal' has, rightly or wrongly, but repeatedly, been attributed – meant that his music absorbed and transformed cultural trends and movements across seven decades while remaining unmistakably and triumphantly itself.

Stravinsky earned his status as a twentieth-century giant at least in part because, one hot spring night in May 1913, three weeks before his thirty-first birthday, he gave the century one of its mythic cultural moments in the Paris premiere of *Le Sacre du printemps – The Rite of Spring*. The scandal of the *Rite*'s riotous first performance has become part of the folklore of modernism, and is one of the most documented artistic events of all time. The moment was not Stravinsky's alone. In the spirit of Sergey Diaghilev's Ballets Russes, the company that brought it to the stage, *The Rite of Spring* was a *Gesamtkunstwerk*, a 'total work of art': a ballet with a scenario, sets and costumes created by the archaeologist and painter Nicholas Roerich and new choreography by the Ballets Russes' sensational star dancer Vaslav Nijinsky. The ballet rode the current Parisian craze for Russianism with its imagined ancient Slavic ritual, the sacrifice of a young girl to the god of spring.

That *The Rite of Spring* appeared in the year 1913 has only added to the power of its mythology. It was a major year for modernism, a time when art, literature and music were wrestling with a world that seemed on the brink of chaos and fragmentation. This was the year in which Gertrude Stein pulled language apart and first told us that 'Rose is a rose is a rose is a rose' and Marcel Proust published the first instalment of À la recherche du temps perdu (*In Search of Lost Time*). Cubism was five years old but Picasso and Georges Braque were continuing to present a fragmented version of the world with multiple simultaneous perspectives.

Sonia Delaunay's *Electric Prisms* paintings from 1913 embraced the speed and energy of technology while, in Russia, Natalia Goncharova's rayonist paintings depicted reality fractured through rays of light. The year 1913 marked the dawn of modernism in the American art world with the International Exhibition of Modern Art at the Armory, New York. Marcel Duchamp's Futuristic *Nude Descending the Staircase, No. 2* created the biggest stir, with one critic describing it as 'the explosion of a shingle factory'.[2] In 1913 the Viennese architect Adolf Loos first published his essay 'Ornament and Crime', a manifesto for the pared-back modern architecture of a brutal century.

This was also a period of dissent in the arts, and the premiere of *The Rite of Spring* was not the first occasion of a high-profile riot at a musical performance in 1913. At the hallowed Musikverein in Vienna on 31 March an event that became known as the *Skandalkonzert* took place. The music of Schoenberg, Berg and Webern had recently cut loose from the moorings of conventional tonality and this fracture with the past proved too much for the audience. Protests drowned out the sound of the orchestra and the concert had to be stopped. And, on 9 March in the Constanzi Theatre in Rome, Luigi Russolo, a painter and composer of the Futurist group, attended a concert of new music that ended in 'fist and cane fighting' between the conservative and progressive factions of the audience. As a reaction, Russolo published a short pamphlet entitled *The Art of Noises* in which he argued for a music in which the sounds of twentieth-century machines, aeroplanes and motorcars would be incorporated into orchestras. This was, after all, the year in which Henry Ford introduced the first motorized assembly line to produce the Model T and Roland Garros flew from the south of France to Tunisia in the first flight across the Mediterranean.

The Rite of Spring announced itself as an ancient ritual but to many who witnessed early performances it was also a picture of the modern world, with all its disclocations and noises and terrors. T. S. Eliot described how Stravinsky had managed 'to transform the rhythm of the steppes into the scream of the motor horn, the rattle of machinery, the grind of the wheels, the beating of iron and steel, the roar of the underground railway and the other barbaric cries of modern life; and to transform these despairing noises into music'.[3] *The Rite* was seen as not only depicting the past and the present, but the future too, a foreboding of the first global mechanized war, which lay but a year in the future. Writers from Jean Cocteau to Modris Eksteins have seen the ritual sacrifice of the young girl as a prophecy of the coming slaughter of a generation of young people. In wartime Paris, the portrait painter Jacques-Émile Blanche heard the sounds of *The Rite* in the sounds of war: 'During the scientific, chemical "cubist" warfare, on nights made terrible by air raids, I have often thought of the *Sacre*.'[4] Although there is nothing to make us think that Stravinsky or his collaborators had war on their minds, there is no denying the unprecedented violence of the music. It was probably louder than any music heard up to that point, and there are passages when it is hard to put the stutter of machine-guns, the rumble of artillery and the whizzing of shells out of our minds.

The Rite of Spring is still, more than a century after its pre-miere in 1913, a violent, mysterious, complex, miraculous work of art that deserves every overworked hyperbole that has been thrown at it. What was once deemed unplayable has become an orchestral showpiece, performed regularly in concert halls. It is choreographed, plundered by other musicians and more analysed than perhaps any other piece of music. It still has the power to shock, and most people who know *The Rite* remember the sensation of hearing it for the first time. It is also, to some extent, unknowable: every musician I speak to about it shares my sensation that, no matter how many times they hear it, they discover new things in it, whole chunks of music or internal workings that they swear weren't there the last time. It is still daunting to listen to and daunting to write about. But, while writing this book I've borne in mind something that Nijinsky, its first choreographer, wrote to Stravinsky during a particularly troubled period in rehearsal before the first performance, something that reminds us all that *The Rite of Spring* is full of beauty as well as terror and that it can be a direct, powerful and revelatory experience for absolutely anybody:

> I know what *The Rite of Spring* will be when everything is as we both want it: new, and, for an ordinary audience member, a jolting impression and emotional experience. For some it will open new horizons flooded with different rays of sun. People will see new and different colours and different lines. All different, new and beautiful.[5]

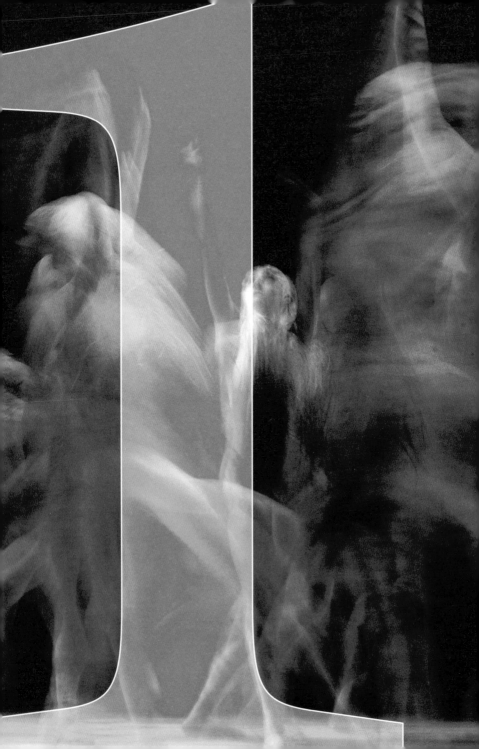

Who was
Igor Stravinsky?

Only three years before the premiere of *The Rite of Spring*, Stravinsky had been a promising but entirely unknown young composer from St Petersburg. When Sergey Diaghilev, impresario of the Ballets Russes, took the risk of commissioning him to write the music for a new ballet, *The Firebird*, for the 1910 Paris season Stravinsky became an overnight sensation. It is often said that his success came out of nowhere, that the sudden emergence of his talent was miraculous. The leap in scale and achievement between his early works and the assured, glittering orchestral score of *The Firebird* was, indeed, remarkable. But Stravinsky's career up until that point reveals that the apparent miracle of *The Firebird* was built on the hard work and determination that were to be a feature of his long working life.

Stravinsky was born on 17 June 1882,* the third of four sons of Fyodor Ignatievich and Anna Kirillovna Stravinsky, in a rented wooden dacha in the holiday resort of Oranienbaum, about fifty kilometres west of St Petersburg. Stravinsky's parents were both descended from minor nobility, their families comprising government officials and modest landowners. His father was a celebrity among the Russian intelligentsia. Fyodor Ignatievich Stravinsky was the leading bass-baritone of the Imperial Opera at St Petersburg's Mariinsky Theatre, recognized as one of the great singer-actors of his age and known in particular for his vivid stage presence in roles such as Varlaam in Mussorgsky's *Boris Godunov* and King Frost in Rimsky-Korsakov's *The Snow Maiden*. It is said that the choice of name for the newest member of the Stravinsky family might have been influenced by the fact that Fyodor had been been in Moscow singing an aria from Borodin's *Prince Igor* just a few days before his son's birth.

The Stravinskys lived in an apartment on the Kryukov Canal

---

* 5 June in the old-style Russian calendar.

in St Petersburg, a stone's throw from the Mariinsky Theatre. An early childhood memory of Stravinsky was of the strange sight of gigantic stage-sets for operas and ballets gliding slowly past the windows of the apartment on canal barges. As an old man, Stravinsky drew from memory a detailed plan of the apartment in which he spent most of his life until the age of twenty-six. The drawing shows the bedroom he shared with his younger brother Gury next door to that of their German nanny. He also carefully drew and labelled two rooms of particular importance to him as a boy and young man: his father's library – one of the best in St Petersburg, so valuable that the Soviet authorities took steps to preserve it after the Revolution – and the drawing room in which two grand pianos sat side by side, a room out of which would emanate the sound of Fyodor learning his operatic roles and in which, later, the young Igor would hammer away at the keyboard for hours, causing his brothers to nickname him 'the piano tuner'.[1]

The composer's most vivid early memories were of sounds. He opens his autobiography with an early sonic memory from a family summer in the country: an 'enormous peasant' sitting on the stump of a tree, singing a two-syllable song and accompanying himself with rapid, rhythmic, armpit-farting noises. Stravinsky reports that his stiffly respectable parents were not amused when he tried to imitate the sound at home. When asked by his collaborator Robert Craft in the late 1950s what he could remember of the St Petersburg of his childhood, he claimed that his most immediate memories were of the sounds of the city: the noise of droshkies (carts) on cobblestones, the scraping of trams as they turned the corner near the apartment, the cries of street vendors selling their wares from the farthest-flung corners of Russia. The conductor Vladimir Jurowski has commented, 'For Stravinsky, the world existed in sound; he regarded the whole universe of sounds, including those written by other people,

overleaf
The young Igor Stravinsky (centre) with his family, Oranienbaum, 1882.

as his workshop.'[2] That is why the sounds of a late nineteenth-century St Petersburg street ended up in his ballet *Petrushka*. And, by a wider process of absorption, it is why the entire history of music seems to have been gathered up and refracted in all of Stravinsky's music.

Stravinsky's memories of childhood were not happy ones and his judgement of his parents was, perhaps unjustifiably, harsh. He said the apartment was gloomy and claustrophobic, his father was bad-tempered, especially on performance days, and his own feelings for his mother did not go beyond duty. 'Childhood', he said, 'was a period of waiting for the moment when I could send everyone and everything connected with it to hell.'[3] But, even if he was not exaggerating, it certainly was not all misery. He took full advantage of his father's library and read greedily. From the age of nine he was given piano lessons and soon discovered that he was a gifted sight-reader, able to play through Fyodor's opera scores, an enviable musical education in itself. He also found a talent for improvisation, for making up music on the spot, for seeking out a musical idea with his fingers and seeing where it would lead him. This was not yet composition, but it was the best possible grounding and, for the rest of his life, Stravinsky was to find his musical ideas at the piano. Outside the home, his mother took him to the opera and ballet round the corner at the Mariinsky. On one memorable occasion when he was ten years old, Anna Kirillovna took him to a gala performance of Glinka's *A Life for the Tsar*. He describes being entranced by the performance and then stepping out into the foyer and seeing the fifty-two-year-old Tchaikovsky standing with his back to him. With his unerring instinct for a good story, the older Stravinsky recalled this incident in the full knowledge that it represented a momentary aligning of the great planets of Russian music. Tchaikovsky was to die just a year later.

Life in the Stravinsky apartment in the long St Petersburg winters was claustrophobic, but escape was available every summer in the form of long and arduous journeys across Russia on trains, riverboats and carriages to spend holidays on the country estates of landowning relatives. One family of cousins, the Nosenkos, had girls to match the Stravinsky boys and lived on an estate at the village of Ustilug at the western extremity of imperial Russia, near the Polish border in Ukraine. From his first visit at the age of eight, Igor was specially drawn to his cousin Yekaterina, finding in this serious, intelligent and sensitive girl the sister he had always longed for.

Stravinsky and his brothers received their early schooling at home, under the supervision of private tutors, which must have added to his sense of incarceration in the Kryukov Canal apartment – or 'Petrushka's Cell' as he later dubbed it. He did not attend school until the age of ten. By his own account, he was an indifferent pupil and his reports suggested that he spent too much time on music: piano lessons, score-reading, improvising and attending the opera. Nonetheless, and presumably to keep his parents happy, he eventually enrolled in the Faculty of Law at St Petersburg University in 1901. At the same time, he was becoming more serious about his musical studies. He knew by now that he wanted to compose and had produced some small pieces. But he felt hampered by his lack of theoretical training: all that improvisation and he did not know how to write any of it down. One of his law student friends was Vladimir Rimsky-Korsakov, son of Nikolai Rimsky-Korsakov, the great composer and professor at the St Petersburg Conservatory. The young Rimsky-Korsakov introduced Stravinsky to his famous father, who recognized raw musical talent in the short and rudimentary pieces that Stravinsky showed him. He advised him to study harmony, counterpoint and orchestration privately. Once he had the basics under his belt, Rimsky-Korsakov intimated, he himself might take Stravinsky on as a private pupil.

That first all-important meeting with Rimsky-Korsakov

took place in Germany, where the Rimsky-Korsakovs and the Stravinskys were spending the summer of 1902. It was common for Russians of their class to pass the summer in the spa towns of Germany, taking the waters, but this holiday had a serious purpose for the Stravinskys: Fyodor was gravely ill with cancer and taking treatment. The cure was unsuccessful and he died in November of that year, at the age of fifty-nine. Nikolai Rimsky-Korsakov quickly became a father figure to Stravinsky; the gatherings of musicians, artists and intellectuals that took place at the Rimsky flat soon became a welcome part of his life. As the fledgling composer applied himself assiduously to music theory (while somehow continuing to study for a law degree), Rimsky-Korsakov's circle broadened Stravinsky's artistic horizon beyond the Kryukov Canal apartment and the Mariinsky Theatre. He attended rehearsals for the Russian symphony concerts put on by the wealthy publisher Mitrofan Belyalev and regular Evenings of Contemporary Music* where he heard the music of foreign composers such as Claude Debussy, Maurice Ravel, Hugo Wolf and Richard Strauss. The young composer was broadening his musical experiences.

In 1905, Stravinsky finished his law course and became a full-time pupil of Nikolai Rimsky-Korsakov. This was a year of revolution and unrest, beginning with a massacre by tsarist troops of unarmed demonstrators in St Petersburg on 'Bloody Sunday' (22 January) and continuing with strikes, demonstrations and uprisings that spread across the entire Russian empire. Rimsky-Korsakov himself was sacked from his Conservatory professorship for publicly supporting the student strikes. As unrest and violence erupted all around him, Stravinsky made the appropriately

---

* A concert series founded in 1902 by Alfred Nurok, Walter Nouvel and Vayacheslav Karatigin.

Nikolai Rimsky-Korsakov, composer and teacher of Igor Stravinsky, 1903.

sympathetic noises of a liberal intellectual. Ultimately, however, he took the view – which was to endure throughout his life – that art was, somehow, above politics. He was energetically throwing himself into writing music, gaining focus and momentum under Rimsky's supervision. A four-movement symphony, which was to occupy him for two years, was the chief result of this period. Performed privately in St Petersburg in 1907, the finished work, in E flat major, has an impeccable – if not very original – late nineteenth-century symphonic structure and strong echoes of Tchaikovsky, Glazunov and Rimsky-Korsakov himself. There was

Igor Stravinsky and his first wife Katya,
St Petersburg, 1907.

little intimation here of the composer of *The Firebird*, much less of *The Rite of Spring*, but Stravinsky's symphony was a great leap forward in the process of becoming a composer.

In 1906, Igor married his first cousin Katya, their relationship raising eyebrows to the extent that the wedding had to be celebrated by a rogue priest on the outskirts of St Petersburg. The couple moved in to the Kryukov Canal apartment with Stravinsky's widowed mother and brothers. In the plan of the apartment from the Robert Craft conversations (*Expositions and Developments*), Stravinsky writes over one of the bedrooms, 'My two oldest children were born here.' By 1908, they were able to build a new house to Stravinsky's design near Katya's family home in Ustilug, a summer retreat with a large first-floor music room where he was to spend periods working on *The Firebird*, *Petrushka* and *The Rite of Spring*.

With a full-scale symphony under his belt, Stravinsky was gaining in confidence and felt able to tackle freer musical forms: the lively, scurrying *Scherzo fantastique* from 1908 is a joyful ten-minute tone poem inspired by Maurice Maeterlinck's essay, 'The Life of Bees', and the even more assured *Fireworks* (*Feu d'artifice*), which followed later the same year, is a sparkling, spinning Catherine wheel for orchestra. The rather earthbound formality of the symphony is gone and we are hearing music that has taken flight: it is extrovert, flexible and – potentially – balletic.

By 1908, Stravinsky's music was being heard in public, and he had gained a publisher. But there was loss too. Rimsky-Korsakov died suddenly of a heart attack on 21 June 1908 at the age of sixty-four, just days after the marriage of his daughter Nadezdka, for whom Stravinsky had composed *Fireworks* as a wedding present. Stravinsky was bereft at losing his beloved teacher and father figure and composed an eleven-minute orchestral work, *Funeral Song*, for a memorial concert in January 1909. The score of this most personal work was missing (Stravinsky attributed this to the chaos of the 1917 Revolution) until 2015 when the orchestral parts were rediscovered during a clear-out of a back room of a library at St Petersburg Conservatory. A new score was made and Stravinsky's memorial to his teacher was given its second performance, 108 years after its first, at the Mariinsky on 2 December 2016.

The newly discovered *Funeral Song* has revealed to the twenty-first century a missing link between the early works and the mastery of the three Diaghilev ballets. The mysterious, creeping opening sounds are closer to the magic and mystery of *The Firebird* than anything we've heard to date. But another new aspect of Stravinsky's composerly voice can now be heard, one that projects beyond *The Firebird*. The music is dark, ceremonial, processional. The orchestra is taking part in an eleven-minute funeral rite with the melody being passed from instrument to instrument as if, in Stravinsky's words, they were 'filing past the tomb of the master in succession, each laying down its own melody as its wreath'.[4] This notion of music as ritual is something new for Stravinsky and will, four years later, be magnified and made terrifying in *The Rite of Spring*.

It's not known if Sergey Diaghilev, impresario and grand exporter of Russian culture, came to Rimsky-Korsakov's memorial concert and heard Stravinsky's *Funeral Song*. But it is certain that, early in 1909, he heard both the *Scherzo fantastique* and *Fireworks* in concerts in St Petersburg and was impressed. He asked Stravinsky to call on him and commissioned him to make two arrangements of Chopin piano pieces for his first Ballets Russes spring season in Paris. This was a straightforward commission that Stravinsky was able to fit in while working on his next big compositional challenge: an opera, *The Nightingale* (usually referred to under its French title as *Le Rossignol*) based on Hans Christian Andersen's story. Stravinsky didn't travel to Paris to hear his orchestrations of Chopin for the ballet *Les Sylphides*

Portrait of Sergei Pavlovich Diaghilev with his Nanny,
by Léon Bakst, 1906.

Sergei Diaghilev, Vaslav Nijinsky and Igor Stravinsky, 1912.

(choreographed by Michel Fokine), but stayed in St Petersburg to work on the opera.

A few months later, there was to be a much more significant interruption. 'A telegram then arrived to upset all my plans,' Stravinsky recalled in his autobiography.[5] Diaghilev urgently needed a composer to write new music for a new Russian ballet for the Ballets Russes' spring 1910 Paris season. Stravinsky, the twenty-seven-year-old Chopin arranger, was Diaghilev's third choice to write the music for *The Firebird*, which was to be the Ballets Russes' first 'total art work', with music, stage design and choreography all newly created and all equally important. Time was short, but Stravinsky accepted the commission, put *The Nightingale* to one side and started work.

The Firebird was intended by Diaghilev to feed the Parisian craze for Russian art and culture which he himself had encouraged, developed and brilliantly exploited. It was to provide Stravinsky with his big break, and this new talent from the Ballets Russes stable seemed, to Paris audiences, to come out of nowhere. But, as we've seen, the industrious Stravinsky had been acquiring skill and knowledge over years back in St Petersburg so that, when his big moment came, he was ready. It had taken him years of hard work to become an overnight success.

The Reinvention
of the Russian Soul

'I have spoken Russian all my life,' Stravinsky told a Moscow journalist in 1962. 'I think in Russian, my way of expressing myself is Russian. Perhaps this is not immediately apparent in my music, but it is latent there, a part of its hidden nature.'[1] In his eightieth year, Stravinsky accepted an invitation from the Soviet authorities to visit his homeland for a tour that included concerts, press appearances and official engagements. He had last set foot on Russian soil in 1914 and, in the intervening five decades, had lived in France, Switzerland and the United States, uprooted by wars, revolution and economic necessity. During those years, he had made no secret of his loathing of the Soviet regime and had refused several official invitations to return. But, eventually, the pull was too strong and the homecoming was, for the notoriously cool and detached Stravinsky, surprisingly emotional.

In acknowledging the hidden Russian nature in his music, Stravinsky had changed his tune. For most of his life he had cultivated the idea that he was the very definition of a cosmopolitan, international modernist; his art was without borders, without any kind of accent, Russian or otherwise. After 1922, he did not set to music a single word of the Russian language. He put on the clothing of a thoroughly Western composer: he wrote neo-classical symphonies and sonatas; a Latin mass and a symphony of psalms; ballets and cantatas on Greek myths; an opera with W. H. Auden; tangos, ragtimes, a jazz concerto and Old Testament settings. Throughout his life, he played down or flatly denied that he borrowed from Russian folk music and was quick to criticize other composers, including Béla Bartók and Leoš Janáček, who had any interest in nationalism or folklorism. And, in the early 1950s, Stravinsky put on the ultimate international modernist garb by adopting a version of Arnold Schoenberg's twelve-tone serialism and making it his own.

Nevertheless, it was impossible for Stravinsky to deny that the music that first made him an international celebrity could not have been more Russian: *The Firebird*, *Petrushka* and *The Rite of Spring* were rooted in his country's myths and folk culture. In his post-First World War music he continued to draw on Russian themes: the *Symphonies of Wind Instruments* (1920) memorialized Debussy in the form of an Orthodox funeral rite; the mini-opera *Mavra* (1922) was based on a comic story by Pushkin, and his ballet music for *Les Noces* (1923) reflected the rituals of a Russian peasant wedding. Stravinsky's sudden fame in his late twenties, ignited by the three great Paris ballets, coincided with – and indeed partly caused – the spectacular climax in the story of a confident Russian culture that had been building for a century and which, for a brief moment just before the Great War, seemed to dominate the arts in Europe.

In the opening scene of *War and Peace*, Tolstoy takes us back to a high-society drawing room in St Petersburg in 1805.[2] A young St Petersburg nobleman takes the floor to tell a story. He switches from the French that everybody at the party is speaking into Russian – because it's 'a Moscow story' – only to flounder in his native language. He spoke, says Tolstoy, 'in such Russian as a Frenchman would speak after spending about a year in Russia'. Tolstoy is poking fun at the young prince but also making the serious point that the Westernized Russian elite had become foreigners in their own land, disconnected from their own language and culture. How to reconnect with a real or imagined Russianness was the predominant theme of Russian literature, painting and music throughout the nineteenth century.

The moment when the thread of Russian culture had broken was traced back to Peter the Great who, at the turn of the eighteenth century, sought to modernize Russia by looking westwards towards the great European cities. Peter travelled to Amsterdam and London to find out about current developments in shipbuilding, science and technology. He enlisted Italian architects to design St Petersburg, his new westward-facing capital city on a marsh drained by canals in the manner of Venice and Amsterdam. He loosened the hold of the ancient Orthodox Church and insisted that the nobility adopt Western habits, banning the beards and traditional dress of old Muscovy. But Peter's modernization project did not go as far as social or political reform; beyond the small Westernized elite, Russia remained a vast, backward, feudal domain stretching from Europe to Asia, reliant on millions of serfs and an impoverished, illiterate peasant class. The essential project of many of the artists of the nineteenth century was to engage in a dialogue between Peter's Westernization and an ancient, possibly mythic idea of Russianness that would unite Europe and Asia, aristocrat and peasant.

As Tolstoy's young prince demonstrates, there was work to be done in finding a language for this cultural resurgence. In the 1820s, Pushkin did for the Russian language what Shakespeare had done for English two hundred years earlier. He created an accessible, literary Russian in which to tell Russian stories, invented new words and put them into the mouths of Russian characters across the entire spectrum of society, and prepared the way for the later explosion of Russian literature with Turgenev, Gogol, Dostoevsky and Tolstoy. The first histories of Russia were written at this time: a vast, twelve-volume *History of the Russian State* by Nikolay Karamzin remained incomplete at his death in 1826. Karamzin's history, passages of which he read aloud to his patron, Tsar Alexander l, in the gardens of the royal palace of Tsarskoye Selo, was a vigorous defence of tsarist autocracy: it told the stories of great men and women, kings and queens; Russia's enormous peasant population was entirely absent. But he was already out of step with a generation of Russian nobility who had fought alongside the peasantry in the Napoleonic wars and could not accept the continuation of the old inequalities. Alienated by what they saw as the artificial stage-set of Westernized, aristocratic St

Petersburg, they sought to live more 'authentic' lives by embracing traditional Russian language, dress and customs.

The leaders of the 1825 Decembrist revolt came from this group, their campaign for constitutional reform and the abolition of serfdom reaching its climax in a confrontation with the tsar's troops in St Petersburg's Senate Square on 26 December of that year. After the crushing of the revolt, many of the Decembrists were exiled to Siberia, where they lived long, active and integrated lives among communities in the far-flung eastern regions of Russia. Far from being forgotten, their exile expanded the notion of what Russia could be, and fixed in the aristocratic Russian imagination an ideal of a purer, simpler, more authentically Russian life. The idea began to take root, chiefly among young aristocratic men, that the huge gulf between aristocrat and peasant could be bridged by a shared idea of a common Russian soul.

Leo Tolstoy originally intended that *War and Peace* would be a Decembrist novel and it retains, at its heart, the longing for a simpler ideal of a Russian existence. It was published in 1869, at the end of a decade that saw both the emancipation of the serfs and a flowering of the arts and intellectual life in Russia. The great novelists Turgenev, Dostoevsky and Tolstoy were at the height of their powers in the 1860s. At the start of the decade, the Mariinsky Theatre opened as a home for Russian opera and ballet. The St Petersburg and Moscow Conservatories were also founded in this decade, providing professional training for Russian musicians for the first time; the twenty-one-year-old Tchaikovsky was one of the first students in St Petersburg. New libraries, ethnographic museums and archives made Russian art, history and literature more widely available than before. It was in the 1860s that the ethnographer Alexander Afanasyev, often compared to the Brothers Grimm in Germany, published collections of Russian folk tales. These stories were to provide inspiration over the coming decades: Rimsky-Korsakov used them for his opera

overleaf
Teremok house on Maria Tenisheva's Talashkino estate, 2013.

The Snow Maiden (1880–81), as did Modest Mussorgsky for his tone poem *Night on a Bare Mountain* (1867), and Diaghilev's Ballet Russes artists went to Afanasyev to find the stories for *The Firebird*. Afanasyev also speculated about ancient Slavic cults and rituals. Among the most potent of these rituals were those around the Slavic god Yarilo, associated with spring, vegetation, fertility and a youthful, violent eroticism. Half a century later, this was to be a key source for *The Rite of Spring*.

Just like the 1960s, the 1860s had its counter-cultural movements. In 1863, a group of fourteen art students staged a walkout at the Imperial Academy of Arts in St Petersburg in protest at the narrow curriculum, focused on Western classical subjects. These painters, led by the hot-headed Ivan Kramskoy, saw the role of the artist as helping to forge an authentic Russian identity through their work. They set up an alternative artistic collective in St Petersburg and began to document Russian life in realistic detail. They painted vivid portraits of Russian artists, such as the intense, nervy evocation of the troubled Dostoevsky by Vasily Perov (1872) or the later image of Mussorgsky by Ilya Repin (1881), painted just days before the composer's alcohol-related death. Russian landscapes and scenes from Russian history were also favourite subjects.

What was perhaps most remarkable was that peasants were often the main subject matter of their paintings, instead of being ancillary figures. In the same way, Turgenev created fully rounded peasant characters in his 1852 short stories *Sketches from a Hunter's Album* and the simple humanity of the peasant Platon in Tolstoy's *War and Peace* provides an important moral touchstone in the novel. Repin's painting *Barge Haulers on the Volga* (1870–73) is a brutally realistic image of a group of men and boys tethered together to pull a riverboat upstream, the pain etched on each individual face and body. It's as devastating a social commentary as anything that Dickens was writing at the time. Determined

Portrait of Vladimir Vasilievich Stasov,
Russian art critic, by Ilya Repin.

that this new Russian art should reach ordinary people, the artists began organizing travelling exhibitions around the far-flung provinces, for which reason the group eventually became known as *Peredvizhniki*: the Wanderers.

One of Ilya Repin's most striking portraits is a 1905 depiction of an impressive-looking elderly man with a long beard, wearing a vivid red peasant tunic. This is no peasant, but the critic, historian and archivist Vladimir Stasov, ferocious campaigner for a Russian national style in the arts and intellectual leader of the *Peredvizhniki*. Stasov was determined that his vision of a true Russian art should also apply to music. By the 1860s, Russia had already had its first major composer with Mikhail Glinka (1804–57), described by the critic Hermann Laroche as 'our musical Pushkin'.[3] Glinka's music, which included the operas *A Life for the Tsar* and *Ruslan and Lyudmila*, based on the Pushkin poem, certainly had Russian themes. But Stasov wanted to push this further. In the 1860s, he acted as a guiding spirit for a group of young composers that had gathered around Mily Balakirev in St Petersburg. Nikolai Rimsky-Korsakov, César Cui, Modest Mussorgsky, Alexander Borodin and Balakirev were, like the *Peredvizhniki* painters, outside the Academy. All of the group apart from Balakirev were amateurs: Rimsky was a teenage naval cadet when he first met Balakirev; Cui was an army engineer; Borodin was a chemist and Mussorgsky a civil servant. The young Tchaikovsky, with his conservatory training, was initially drawn to Balakirev's circle, but eventually settled for a respectful distance, suspicious of their studied 'untutored' character and wearing his own Russianness more lightly. But Stasov wanted the world to know that there was now a truly Russian school of composers. So, in 1867, he gave this little group a title: the *Moguchaya Kuchka*: the Mighty Handful.

In their search for an authentically Russian voice, folk music was fruitful raw material for the *Kuchka* composers: Balakirev spent several summers in the 1860s travelling down the River Volga collecting folk songs. While Tchaikovsky was embarking on a career writing symphonies (as well as operas and ballets), some containing Russian folk tunes, Stasov increasingly believed that new musical forms were needed for this new Russian music The tendency of the *Kuchka* was to pull away from Germanic symphonic form and towards free-flowing structures suggested by storytelling. Rimsky's tone poem *Sadko* and Mussorgsky's terrifying *Night on a Bare Mountain* were early examples. The subject matter, whether mythical or historic, was invariably Russian. Like the *Predvizhniki* painters, the *Kuchka* composers liked to transpose real life into art. In his *Pictures at an Exhibition*, Mussorgsky's *Bydło* creates an almost filmic depiction of a lumbering ox cart as it laboriously clanks and rattles past and into the distance, while Balakirev's short and fiendishly difficult piano piece *Islamey* (subtitled 'Oriental Fantasy') captures a moment during a trip to the Caucasus when a folk musician played a fast fiddle tune to him. The *Kuchka* composers, encouraged by Stasov, embraced an Asiatic view of Russia that was to prove highly exportable for Diaghilev's Ballets Russes and was to live on in twentieth-century popular culture as a shorthand for a kind of perfumed orientalism. A sinuous melody from Rimsky's opera *Sadko* became 'Song of India', a popular jazz standard in the 1930s, and Borodin's memorable tunes from his unfinished opera *Prince Igor* provided the score for the 1950s Broadway musical *Kismet*. Asia by way of St Petersburg.

As the nineteenth century progressed, a new class of people became crucial players in the arts in Russia. Wealthy individuals who had made their fortunes in industry and transport infrastructure lent their financial weight to the push for an authentically Russian culture. In 1870, the railway magnate Savva Mamontov set up an artists' colony at Abramtsevo, his estate north of Moscow. Leading Russian artists, including some of the *Peredvizhniki* painters, worked at Abramtsevo, and Mamontov's Private Opera Company, an alternative to the imperial theatres, staged operas by *Kuchka* composers. The growing cult of peasant

Barge Haulers on the Volga (1870–3), by Ilya Repin.

THE RITE OF SPRING

arts and crafts was also nurtured at Abramtsevo with workshops creating ceramics, textiles and furniture, all of which proved highly marketable to a growing middle class. These artefacts included the *matryoshka*, the famous Russian nesting dolls that were readily believed at home and abroad to be an authentic example of traditional Russian peasant art. This was, in fact, an adaptation of a Japanese design and was invented at Abramtsevo by the artist Sergey Malyutin in 1890.

Abramtsevo was a breeding ground for the ideas that were eventually to lead to the Ballets Russes and *The Rite of Spring*, as was a similar enterprise set up in 1893 by the Princess Maria Tenisheva at Talashkino, near Smolensk. Tenisheva had married into wealth derived from railways and river steamers and, like Mamontov, she set out to preserve the peasant arts and crafts traditions that were threatened by the very industrialization that had created her fortune.* In the workshops at Talashkino local people could learn traditional crafts. Later she self-deprecatingly described the peasant women's distaste at the dull, sludgy colours of the 'traditional' vegetable dyes the well-meaning princess was promoting. But the Talashkino project had wider ambitions than philanthropy and a traditional craft revival. The princess saw in these Russian traditions, real or imagined, a source for innovative art on the international stage. Tenisheva became a key figure, both financially and philosophically, in the circle of the Ballets Russes. It was to Talashkino that Stravinsky and his collaborator Nicholas Roerich came in 1910 to work on the idea for *The Rite of Spring*. The Stravinsky–Roerich ballet, with its potential for a startling modernity born of ancient Russian roots, must have seemed like the perfect Talashkino project.

Stravinsky and Roerich had met in 1904 through their

---

* She had married the manufacturer Prince Vyacheslav Nikolayevich Tenishev in 1892.

involvement in the magazine *Mir iskusstva* ('The World of Art') and its circle of St Petersburg artists under the patronage of Princess Tenisheva and the artistic leadership of the young critic and impresario Sergey Diaghilev. This confident generation saw itself as the vanguard of Russian artistic renewal. Cosmopolitan, elite, free-thinking, these young aesthetes had little patience with the nationalist, socially engaged realism of the Stasov years but believed rather in art for art's sake, the pursuit of beauty as an end in itself and modern artistic trends including art nouveau and Symbolism. The group, which included the painters Alexandre Nikolayevich Benois, Léon Bakst and Ivan Bilibin, published the magazine and mounted exhibitions. An offshoot of the group presented the Evenings of Contemporary Music where the young Stravinsky heard new music from France and Germany and which, in 1907, provided him with his first public performance. At first, these young cosmopolitan artists were dismissive of the Russian folk revival and, especially, of the folklorism and what they regarded as the crude realism of the nineteenth-century Russian revival. But Diaghilev, with Princess Tenisheva, eventually realized that this connection to a deep Russian past could, in the hands of the right artists, become an eminently exportable form of modern Russian art. The inclusion of the archaeologist, ethnographer and painter Roerich in the *Mir iskusstva* circle connected it to an even more ancient history. Roerich brought his knowledge of prehistoric Russian civilizations, in particular that of the Scythians, nomadic tribes who roamed the steppe from Central Asia to the Black Sea. In 1897, Roerich was involved in an archaeological dig of a Scythian burial mound and was captivated by the eloquent primitivism of the artefacts. This found its way into his own painting and, ultimately, the scenario and design for *The Rite of Spring*.

The painter Jacques-Émile Blanche, writing in the *Revue de*

Woman in a turban, by Paul Poiret:
from *Items by Paul Poiret as seen by Georges Lepape*, 1911.

Paris of 1913 after five Ballets Russes seasons, tells us just how right Tenisheva and Diaghilev had been about the appetite for this particular version of Russian culture. Paris had gone mad for it: 'The dress of our wives and children, the furnishings and the novelty shops have been taken over by the "gout Russe".'[4] As one Ballets Russes season followed another, the audience increasingly became a mirror of the stage as prosperous Parisian women adopted the Ballets Russes-inspired clothes being turned out by the top fashion houses.

As early as 1909, the *New York Times* reported that the Rue de la Paix, the chief thoroughfare of Paris fashion, was a riot of 'strong Russian colours, reds and orange and green' of the 'Russian and barbaric costumes' that were all the rage. The loose-fitting Russian blouse featured in several collections, and fur was an essential addition to these 'Siberian novelties'. The prestigious Redfern boutique in particular was, the *Times* continued, like an outpost of St Petersburg, the doorman being 'a tall Russian boy, in a native costume... with brilliant complexion, red blouse, high boots and a Cossack cap in Persian wool'. The couturier Paul Poiret, reflecting the Asiatic tendency of the Ballets Russes, dressed his Parisian clients in turbans, harem pants and floating tunics inspired by the orientalist fantasies of *Sheherezade* (a ballet adaptation of an orchestral suite by Rimsky-Korsakov, premiered at the Opéra Garnier by the Ballets Russes on 4 June 1910) and Stravinsky's *Firebird*. In 1912, the couturière Jeanne Paquin enlisted Ballets Russes designer Léon Bakst to help her design a collection of day dresses, taking the Russian style from the stage on to the streets of Paris. Paris boutiques did a roaring trade in Russian folk textiles and artefacts including, of course, the *matryoshka*.

The Parisian enthusiasm for Russian culture had been building for a decade or so before the Ballets Russes came to town, and Diaghilev and his immediate circle should be credited for much of it. Diaghilev's patron, the Princess Tenisheva, was a guiding force behind the Russian Pavilion at the 1900 Paris Exposition Universelle, which also included a huge, fantasy Kremlin built near the Seine, a chance to experience a virtual journey on the new Trans-Siberian Railway and a life-sized reconstruction of a Russian village. There was much excitement around town about the influx of real Russian peasants with real beards and smocks who had come to build the village and provide the living characters. The *matryoshka* dolls also made an impact, winning a bronze medal for design.

In 1906, Diaghilev mounted his first Parisian venture, an exhibition entitled 'Two Centuries of Russian Painting and Sculpture', as part of the Salon d'Automne, an annual showcase for avant-garde and progressive art. Diaghilev presented the French public with 750 works, telling the hitherto untold story of Russian art. The success of the exhibition made Diaghilev a Parisian cultural celebrity: he was, according to a letter from the Princess Tenisheva to Roerich, 'now whirling amid the highest society'.[5] That society included the Countess Greffulhe, fashion tastemaker, muse of Marcel Proust and subsequent supporter of Diaghilev's Paris enterprises. It was at Greffulhe's salon that Diaghilev was introduced to the theatre manager Gabriel Astruc, who was to present all but one of his subsequent Russian seasons in Paris including, in 1913, *The Rite of Spring*.

The success of the 1906 exhibition and the patronage of Countess Greffuhle emboldened Diaghilev to mount a season of five 'Historic Concerts of Russian Music' the following year at the Paris Opéra. These concerts brought the big names of Russian music to Paris: Glazunov, Rimsky-Korsakov and Rachmaninov conducted their own music, and Rachmaninov also played his greatest hit, the Second Piano Concerto. The great Russian bass Feodor Chaliapin was first introduced to the Paris public in these concerts, singing music by Mussorgsky and Borodin. Chaliapin was the star of Diaghilev's hugely ambitious production of Mussorgsky's opera *Boris Godunov* in May 1908, which attempted to bring sixteenth-century Russia alive on the Paris stage. Mounted at the Opéra Garnier, this first performance of the opera outside Russia featured crowd scenes involving hundreds of people, sumptuous costumes and sets by the Russian artists Golovin and Bilibin dressed with authentic folk artefacts found in the Princess Tenisheva's collections and, in the words of Benois, by scouring 'the Tatar junk-shops of St Petersburg'.[6] According to Serge Lifar, Paris went wild for Diaghilev's *Boris*:

> The effect it produced on Paris was indescribable. The usual cold and fashionable audience of the Opéra was utterly transformed. People stood on their seats, yelled as if possessed, waved handkerchiefs and wept in an unrestrained and Asiatic manner very different from European tears. Europe had taken Mussorgsky and his *Boris Godunov* to heart![7]

At the same time as Diaghilev was consciously building the audience for the great men of the arts from Russia, the Princess Tenisheva was promoting the *goût russe* among the women of Paris. Two lengthy features about her collections of and support for Russian folk arts and crafts appeared in *Femina*, the sophisticated cultural magazine for women. In 1907, she held an exhibition at the Louvre entitled 'The Russian Decorative Arts', which showcased her collections of traditional Russian arts and artefacts, from icons to peasant costumes.

The synthesis of the arts was an important element of the success of the 1908 production of *Boris Godunov*: Russian visual artists of the highest calibre worked alongside musicians to create a scenic and musical spectacle. Ballet was the ultimate synthetic art form and Diaghilev, recognizing a market for it, resolved to create a dance company and bring it to Paris in 1909. 'I had already presented Russian painting, Russian music, Russian opera in Paris,' he proclaimed. 'Ballet contains all of these.' The idea of

overleaf
Set design for the prologue of Alexander Borodin's
Prince Igor, by Konstantin Korovin.

the *Gesamtkunstwerk*, the total work of art, was associated with Richard Wagner, a hero of the *Mir iskusstva* artists, but Diaghilev managed to reinvent it as an essentially Russian notion and it became the guiding principle of his new company, the Ballets Russes. Writing after the premiere of *The Rite of Spring* in 1913, the critic Jacques Rivière would put his finger on what he regarded as the primal, mystical and particularly Russian communion of minds behind this synthesis of the arts:

> Who is the author of *Le Sacre du printemps*? Who created it? Nijinsky, Stravinsky or Roerich? That preliminary question which we cannot evade is meaningful only to Westerners such as we. With us, everything is individual: all of our fine and characteristic works always bear the mark of a single mind. This is not the case with the Russians. Although they cannot communicate with us, among themselves they have an extraordinary ability to meld their souls, to feel and think the same thing collectively. Their race is still too young for all those thousands of little idiosyncrasies to have developed in each man, those delicate personal reticences, those thin but impenetrable membranes which guard the threshold of the cultivated mind.[8]

Diaghilev was not in a position to form a permanent dance company for the 1909 Paris season but, back in St Petersburg, he went to the Imperial Ballet looking for dancers, who were only too happy to spend their holidays moonlighting on an new exciting project: the pay was better, they got to travel abroad and to rub shoulders with painters and designers such as Bakst, Benois and Roerich in the rehearsal room. The May 1909 cover of the Parisian arts magazine *Comœdia* announced the new *Saison Russe* with an image in watercolour and gold paint of the prima ballerina Tamara Karsavina drawn and sumptuously costumed by Léon Bakst. The costume was a kind of prototype Firebird, the golden bird from *Le Festin*, a ballet suite put together for the 1909

Léon Bakst's costume design for the Firebird, 1909.

season with music by Rimsky-Korsakov, Glinka, Tchaikovsky and Glazunov. Diaghilev had recognized that the Paris audience wanted full-scale exoticism and untamed 'otherness' from the Russians and they got it, perhaps most memorably in the *Polovtsian Dances* from Borodin's *Prince Igor*, choreographed by Fokine with richly coloured sets by Roerich depicting the Central Asian steppe. Victor Seroff provides a vivid account of this testosterone-fuelled spectacle:

> As if to show the civilized Europeans what the true Asia can look like, the Russian painters produced a stage setting of such fantastic colours that no splendour of the Orient, familiar through fables, could surpass the picture that was offered to the audience. And when, in addition to this background and Borodin's exotic and powerful music, a horde of wild tatars were seen on the stage dancing, leaping over each other with their unsheathed curved sabres slicing the air, it is not surprising that the audience rushed forward at the end of the dancing and actually tore down the orchestra rail to clasp the performers in their arms.[9]

Adding to the thrill, Diaghilev had put a new generation of young principal dancers on the Paris stage. These included Tamara Karsavina and Nijinsky, whose physical power and gravity-defying leaps – he seemed to be able to freeze in mid-air – surpassed anything that had been seen before. But Parisian critics were united in the view that the 1909 season had not produced any music to match the freshness and innovation of the dance and stage design. All the music was pre-existing; it was a cobbled-together mix of extracts and arrangements of Russian masters and second-rate composers and, for *Les Sylphides*, a compilation of Chopin piano pieces arranged by Russian composers including Glazunov, Lyadov and a young unknown named Igor Stravinsky. If they were to continue to impress, Diaghilev's company must commission a major new ballet with original music for the 1910

Léon Bakst's costume design for the Princess in *The Firebird*, 1910.

season, a work that would ride the wave of the Russian nationalist craze. That work was *The Firebird*.

The Firebird was to be the perfect *Mir iskusstva Gesamtkunstwerk*. The scenario was drawn up by committee, a group of artists in the Ballets Russes circle, headed by the ethnographically meticulous Benois. It was to be a blending of several Slavic folk tales and recurrent mythic characters: the evil wizard Kashchei, who menaced young women and who is immortal unless an egg hidden in a casket containing his soul can be smashed; Ivan Tsarevich, the stock hero of many Russian folk tales; and the Firebird herself: noble, magical, opulently plumed, who flies in from a land far away to intervene in human lives. Choreography was to be by Fokine; the fantastical, Asiatic costumes by Bakst; the rich and elaborately painted sets by Golovin, and there was to be a newly commissioned musical score. Diaghilev had made several false starts in finding a composer to match these artists before eventually deciding to take a risk on his twenty-seven-year-old Chopin arranger Stravinsky. It was a bold move, but Diaghilev immediately started to build the hype for his new star, introducing him to the dancers with the words, 'Mark him well. He is a man on the brink of celebrity.' He also made sure that, for the premiere of *The Firebird*, the rich and fashionable were joined by artists, writers and musicians eager to find out about the young composer Diaghilev was proposing as the equal of Fokine, Benois, Bakst and Golovin. Stravinsky's music for *The Firebird* was composed in only six months in close collaboration with Fokine and showed a precocious mastery of dramatic storytelling as well as glittering orchestral colour and a well-judged use of folk melodies. *The Firebird*'s music had much that was familiar to the Parisians who had heard Mussorgsky and Rimsky-Korsakov in previous seasons – indeed, Stravinsky borrowed some folk tunes and harmonic techniques from his teacher* – but, amid the folk tunes, dances and sumptuous orchestration, a sharp gleam of modernity shone through. Diaghilev's gamble had paid off and the mission of the Ballets Russes had finally crystallized.

The first night of *The Firebird*, on 25 June 1910 at the gilded Opéra Garnier in Paris, was to change Stravinsky's life overnight. The young composer from St Petersburg was thrust into what felt like the centre of the cultural universe: he remembered being feted by major figures including Sarah Bernhardt, Jean Cocteau, Maurice Ravel, Claude Debussy, André Gide and the socialites the Comtesse Greffuhle and the Princesse de Polignac. *The Firebird*'s sensational success meant that he was immediately embraced as one of them, his name mentioned for evermore when the Paris of those times is evoked. The choreographer Fokine and the designers Benois and Golovin were familiar to Paris audiences from the previous season, but Stravinsky was a talent that seemed to have appeared from nowhere. The premiere of *The Firebird* was also the moment when Stravinsky became an international figure and the start – although he did not know it yet – of a permanent separation from his Russian homeland. For the time being, Stravinsky took it all in his stride.

Diaghilev followed the success of *The Firebird* with a second Stravinsky–Fokine commission for the following season. The set and costumes were again by Benois, but the version of Russianness in *Petrushka* was altogether more down to earth. There was none of *The Firebird*'s exotic plumage and whiff of the orient. This was a vivid picture of Russian life, a street scene depicting the St Petersburg Shrovetide Fair with hawkers, peasant farmers, wet nurses, street musicians, a performing bear and a puppet show.

---

* A notable borrowing from Rimsky-Korsakov in *The Firebird* is the use of the so-called octatonic scale (see Chapter 5, page 78) to signify the sorcery of Kashchei.

Against this backdrop was told the story of the tragic fairground anti-hero Petrushka, danced by Nijinsky, and his fatal love triangle with the Princess and the Moor, stock fairground puppet characters brought to life in the ballet by an evil puppet master. The score is packed full of folk tunes, street songs, hawkers' cries and Russian dances – the sounds of Stravinsky's St Petersburg childhood – and he even borrowed a popular Parisian music-hall song ('Elle avait une jambe en bois'), which he'd heard on a barrel organ in the street below his apartment. But among all this realism, and especially in the crunching dissonances of the so-called *Petrushka* chord, associated with the puppet's tragedy, there are seeds of the innovations to come in *The Rite of Spring*.

Alexandre Benois' costume design for the Ballerina in *Petrushka*, 1911.

From a Dream to a First Night: The Making of *The Rite of Spring*

One day when I was finishing the last pages of *The Firebird* in St Petersburg, I had a fleeting vision which came to me as a complete surprise, my mind at the moment being full of other things. I saw in imagination a solemn pagan rite: sage elders, seated in a circle, watched a young girl dance herself to death. They were sacrificing her to propitiate the god of spring.[1]

Among the many stories and myths surrounding *The Rite of Spring*, perhaps the most vexed question is about where the idea came from in the first place. Stravinsky's claim, that his most famous work came to him out of nowhere as a fully formed, detailed vision in a dream, is often cited as another example of the composer's relaxed relationship with the truth. As the musicologist Richard Taruskin memorably said, 'Stravinsky spent the second half of his long life telling lies about the first half'.[2]

But even Taruskin concedes that such a dream might not have been so unlikely an event for a young artist in St Petersburg in 1910, when the air was full of ideas about making a new, modern art by connecting with the deep past of Russia, and those ideas were proving to be both artistically fruitful and highly exportable. *The Firebird*, which was just about to be staged by the Ballets Russes in Paris when the alleged dream occurred, was a glittering, bejewelled and sumptuously costumed evocation of magic and folk tales from a fantastical version of Russia, with richly coloured music that Stravinsky's teacher Rimsky-Korsakov would have recognized. Stravinsky's new dream of old Russia was something altogether darker, and reached far more deeply into an ancient, archaeological past.

Stravinsky's story about the dream was hotly contested by the artist who, on the printed score and in all the contemporary press advertisements and programmes, is credited equally with Stravinsky as co-creator: the painter, archaeologist and leading light of *Mir iskusstva,* Nicholas Roerich. For the rest of his life, Roerich claimed that the idea for *The Rite* had originated entirely with him. This is his version of how it happened:

> I don't know what dreams Stravinsky had or when he had them, but this is how it really was: in 1909 Stravinsky came out to see me with a proposal to create a ballet together. After some reflection, I offered him two ballets - one was 'The Rite of Spring'... the other was 'A Game of Chess'.[3]

It seems clear, if Roerich's version of the story is to be believed, that the 'Game of Chess' idea would have stood little chance with the Stravinsky of 1910, intoxicated as he was by Russian culture and folklore; but it tantalizingly pre-echoes a much later ballet, *Jeu de cartes* (*Game of Cards*), which Stravinsky made with George Balanchine for New York a quarter of a century later.

The truth about the origins of *The Rite of Spring* is, predictably, likely to lie somewhere between the conflicting versions of Stravinsky and Roerich, and it is revealing to look at what claims the composer was making about his inspiration at the time. In December 1912, as he was putting the finishing touches to the score of *The Rite of Spring* in a hotel in Clarens, Switzerland, Stravinsky expressed his inspiration in more modest terms in a letter to his friend the journalist Nicolai Findeizen about his new 'choreodrama', giving it its deliciously resonant Russian name:

> My first thought about my new choreodrama *Vesna svyashchennaya* came to me as I was finishing *The Firebird*, spring 1910. I wanted to compose the libretto together with N. K. Roerich, because who else could help me, who else knows the secret of our ancestors' close feeling for the earth? In a few days we worked out the libretto.[4]

So, if Stravinsky had an idea that he wanted to make a 'choreodrama' about the ancient Russian's feeling for the earth then he had, indeed, gone to the right man. Roerich was immediately able to fill in the detail, give colour and form and historical accuracy to this vision because he was already immersed in these ideas himself; and Stravinsky would have known this. Roerich's paintings in the decade preceding his collaboration with Stravinsky are preoccupied with pre-Christian Slavic civilizations, their bright, flat colours chosen to help the viewer imagine what Roerich regarded as a simpler, purer time. As early as 1901, Roerich produced a canvas he called *The Idols* in which a circle of totem poles and wooden monoliths topped by horses' skulls mark out a site of Slavic pagan ritual or sacrifice. Roerich said of *The Idols*, 'It's strong, vivid, there's no drama in it, no sentimentality, but there is a robust pagan mood.'[5] This could be Stravinsky talking about his pagan ballet from a decade later: 'There are simply no regions for soul searching in *The Rite of Spring*.'[6]

A vision even closer to the world of *The Rite of Spring* is found in Roerich's writings: in his vivid imagining of a pagan ritual found in the 1908 essay 'Joy in Art', written two years before Stravinsky's alleged dream. Here he imagines the birth of art itself, coming quite naturally out of the customs and habits of a community of people:

> A Festival. Let it be the festival at which they always celebrated the victory of the spring sun. They would go into the forests for a long time, admiring the colour of the trees; they would make fragrant wreaths from the first herbs and adorn themselves with them. They would dance rapid dances when they wanted to be liked. They would play on horns and pipes of bone and wood. Garments would mingle in the crowd, garments full of fur edgings and woven colours. Beautiful wicker and skin shoes would step out. The *khorovod*s [traditional round dances] would gleam with amber pendants, tabs, stone beads and while talismans made from teeth. The people would rejoice. Art was beginning among them.[7]

With hindsight, Roerich's description reads like the beginnings of a scenario for *The Rite of Spring* five years before it was put on the stage, complete with ideas for music, dance, costumes and props. But it also chimes with Stravinsky's rapidly changing thoughts about theatre and dance at the time. He had become excited by new theories about drama and movement, in particular by the recent writings of the German stage director Georg Fuchs who, in his book *Revolution in the Theatre*, proposed an anti-naturalistic, ritual type of theatre, getting back in touch with ancient festivals and community rites, softening the boundaries between the audience and the stage. Whereas, with his first two ballets, *The Firebird* and *Petrushka*, Stravinsky told stories through characters and dramatic situations, he already knew that the new work would be different. The choreography would be dominated by the movement of masses of people on the stage, groups and communities rather than solo characters. The new ballet would not tell the story of a ritual; it would, in itself, be that ritual.[8]

The first discussions about this new project, which was given the working title 'The Great Sacrifice', took place in summer 1910, around the time when Stravinsky and the Ballets Russes were having huge success with *The Firebird* in Paris. At that stage, the creative players in 'The Great Sacrifice' were Stravinsky, Roerich and Fokine, the choreographer of *The Firebird* and lead choreographer of the Ballets Russes. They were working out the beginnings of a scenario, and Roerich gave the following summary to the *Petersburg Gazette*, a first, tentative description of the new work:

> The action takes place on the summit of a sacred hill, before
> dawn. It begins on a summer night and ends before sunrise,
> when the first rays appear. The piece will be the first attempt to
> give a re-creation of antiquity without a specific dramatic plot.[9]

It's clear that Diaghilev, usually the master of ceremonies for all ideas and collaborations in the Ballets Russes company, had not been involved in either the idea nor in the initial creative discussions about the new project – and he was not best pleased. Stravinsky wrote to his co-conspirator Roerich while still in Paris just after the *Firebird* premiere:

> Naturally the success of *The Firebird* has encouraged Diaghilev for future projects, and sooner or later we will have to tell him about 'The Great Sacrifice'. In fact, he has already asked me to compose a new ballet. I said I was writing one which, for the moment, I did not wish to talk about, and this touched off an explosion, as I might have guessed. 'What? You keep secrets from me, I who do my utmost for you all? Fokine, you, everyone has secrets from me!'[10]

If Diaghilev's nose was put out of joint, his instincts as producer and impresario must soon have helped him sense that the combination of ideas and personalities involved in 'The Great Sacrifice' could spectacularly achieve what the Ballets Russes was becoming known for in the great cities of Europe: an alchemical mix of fashionable Russian exoticism and cutting-edge modernity. He got behind the project and scheduled it to premiere in the 1912 Paris season. Meanwhile, as a post-*Firebird* holiday, Stravinsky took his wife and three children from Paris to the busy Breton seaside resort of La Baule, which, he wrote, was 'crowded with children of all ages'. There he took walks and swam in the sea with his family, but his mind was clearly still racing with ideas about the new project. He wrote to Roerich, also on a seaside holiday in the resort of Hapsal on the Baltic coast: 'I am impatient for news. . . Please write your address legibly because I have no idea where to find you, and I have much to say about our future child'. And, as a postscript, by way of encouragement, 'I have started work (sketches) on "The Great Sacrifice". Have you done anything for it yet?'[11]

But the boot was soon on the other foot. Stravinsky took his family to Switzerland for the winter and became sidetracked by a new project that had grabbed his interest, the ballet *Petrushka*.

The premiere was scheduled for the 1911 Ballets Russes season with Nijinsky in the title role and Stravinsky had his work cut out. He sent an apologetic message to Roerich through Benois:

> He [Roerich] shouldn't get angry, since I've never had any intention of putting 'The Great Sacrifice' on the back burner, and will compose it just as soon as *Petrushka* is finished. I would never have finished 'The Great Sacrifice' before April anyway. That was the deadline Diaghilev gave me.[12]

As soon as *Petrushka* had been premiered in Paris in June 1911, Stravinsky was urging Roerich to get the ball rolling again with 'The Great Sacrifice'. 'I feel it is imperative that we see each other to decide about every detail – especially every question of staging – concerning our child,' he wrote. 'I expect to start composing in the autumn and, health permitting, I hope to finish in the spring.'[13] And where better for them to see each other and start plotting their ancient Russian ritual in earnest than at the Talashkino estate, the artists' colony near Smolensk set up by the enlightened arts patron the Princess Tenisheva? Here, at one of the nerve centres of the Russian Revival movement, the two artists would be able to breathe the very air of ancient Russia. When he arrived at Talashkino after the long train journey from his own country estate in Ustilug, Stravinsky was housed with Roerich in a 'colourful fairy house', one of several buildings at Talashkino the Princess had commissioned in a fantastical Russian style. To add to the mood, he describes being waited on by servants dressed in white costumes with red belts and black boots.[14] Around the estate, the composer would have come across furniture and wall friezes on Scythian themes designed by his collaborator Roerich, coloured with vegetable dyes made on the estate following traditional methods and, most spectacular of all, the Church of the Descent of the Holy Spirit, a recently built elaborate Russian fantasy for which Roerich had designed the external mosaics and a mystical altar painting entitled *The Heavenly Queen at the River of Life*. One of their fellow guests at Talashkino was the folk singer and *gusli*-player Sergey Kolosov, who accompanied himself as he sang folk songs in the evenings.

In this fertile environment, the two artists set to work on the big idea. Stravinsky reported that Roerich began to sketch his backdrops for the ballet on this visit, as well as making a start on some costume designs, inspired by the Princess's collections of peasant costumes. The most important thing of all was to agree the scenario, the mood, the setting, the shape, form and length of the ballet. This would give Stravinsky the vital framework for his next year of work in writing the music. 'I set to work with Roerich', said Stravinsky, 'and in a few days the plan of action and the titles of the dances were composed.'

We know that when Roerich arrived at Talashkino, he already had the beginnings of a scenario, with his image of an ancient spring festival described so vividly in 'Joy in Art' three years earlier. Scholars have speculated about the possible sources for Roerich's vision of a ritual of spring. In his 1869 book *The Poetic Outlook of the Slavs on Nature*, Afanasyev describes a festival in honour of the spring god Yarilo, which, minus the white horse, contains many elements that ended up on stage in *The Rite of Spring*: the groups of young maidens, a chosen girl, *khorovods** and a group of elders looking on:

> In honour of [Yarilo] the Byelorussians celebrate the first sowing
> season [at the end of April] for which purpose maidens are
> rounded up in the villages, and one of them having been
> chosen, she is dressed up exactly as Yarilo is in the imagination
> of the folk, and she is seated on a white horse. Around the
> chosen one in a *khorovod* coils in single file. All who take part

---

*   An ancient slavic dance, traditionally with singing.

in the ritual must wear a wreath of live flowers. If the weather is warm and clear, the ceremony culminates in the open field, in the newly sown cornfield in the presence of the elders.[15]

What is missing from all of the rites of spring described by Afanasyev, Roerich or, indeed, any other chronicler of the ancient Slavs is Stravinsky's idea of a dance to the death. There was no evidence that human sacrifice was part of the rituals of old Russia, but it must have seemed an irresistible idea to a composer who already had an unerring sense of what would create impact in theatre and music. Perhaps this performative twist was, ultimately, Stravinsky's unique contribution to the dramaturgy of *The Rite of Spring*. What could be a more spectacular, a more extreme, a more modern climax to a ballet than a dance to the death?

During their time at Talashkino, Stravinsky and Roerich agreed that their rite would be about half an hour long and would be divided into two balancing scenes, the first set at daybreak, the second during the night. The first scene would be made up of seven dances, the second would have five, and each scene would open with an introduction for orchestra alone, during which the curtain would be down. During the months that followed the Talashkino meeting, Stravinsky and Roerich each gave accounts of what they had decided in Princess Tenisheva's fairy house. While they might have emphasized different aspects of the work, their accounts were broadly in agreement, and the following is an attempt at a distillation of what they said and wrote about the scenario:

Part 1:
The Adoration of the Earth
(or *The Kiss of the Earth* in Russian)
The first scene transports us to the foot of a sacred hill, amid green fields, where Slavonic tribes have gathered for their vernal

games. The orchestral introduction is a swarm of spring pipes (*dudki*). There is an old Sorceress clad in squirrel skins, who performs auguries, looking for signs of the coming of spring in the earth by divining with twigs; the men perform a game of abducting a wife; there is a spring *khorovod* (circle dance) and a game of rival tribes. Finally the most important moment arrives: from the village they bring the Sage, the Oldest and Wisest, so that he might plant his sacred kiss on the flowering earth. The first part closes with a wild, stomping dance upon the earth, the people drunk with spring.

Part 2: The Sacrifice
After this vivid terrestrial rejoicing, in the second scene we proceed to a celestial mystery. The maidens at night perform their mysterious and secret games and rituals on a sacred hillock. One of the maidens is doomed by fate to be sacrificed. She wanders into a stone labyrinth from which there is no exit; the remaining maidens glorify the Chosen One in a boisterous martial dance. Then the Elders enter; they are wearing bearskins as the bear is considered the forefather of humankind. They will give the victim up to the sun god Yarilo. The doomed one, left alone face to face with the elders, dances her last 'sacred dance', the great sacrifice. The leaders are witness to her last dance.[16]

Bar some minor reordering, this version of the scenario remained essentially unchanged from the meeting in Talashkino until the Paris premiere in May 1913. The shape of the ballet was fixed. And one more major decision was taken at Talashkino. 'The Great Sacrifice' was dropped as the title for the work and it was hitherto known as V*esna svyashchennaya*: *The Rite of Spring*.

Before Stravinsky left Talashkino, the Princess Tenisheva insisted that he write some bars of music on the painted beams of the multicoloured guest house in which he had been staying.[17] We shall never know what he wrote as many of the Talashkino buildings were vandalized or destroyed after the Revolution. But we do know that Stravinsky's colourful, primeval experience was not yet over. On the train journey back to Ustilug, Stravinsky describes missing a connection:

> I therefore bribed the conductor of a freight train to let me ride in a cattle car, though I was all alone in it with a bull! The bull was leashed by a single not-very-reassuring rope, and as he glowered and slavered I began to barricade myself behind my one small suitcase. I must have looked an odd sight [. . .] as I stepped from that corrida carrying my expensive (or, at least, not tramp-like) bag and brushing my clothes and hat, but I must have looked relieved.[18]

With all the big artistic questions agreed at Talashkino, Stravinsky needed to sort out the business matters before finally sitting down to compose *The Rite of Spring*. So he was soon back on a train, this time to the Czech spa town of Karlsbad where he met Diaghilev and signed a contract for a commission fee of 4,000 roubles. Then it was on to Berlin to agree terms for *The Rite of Spring* with his publisher, and then back to his estate at Ustilug to start the major task of packing up the family home before leaving to spend the winter at Clarens on the eastern shore of Lake Geneva. At Clarens, he believed that his wife's and children's delicate lungs would benefit from the clean mountain air and that he himself would be able to find the peace of mind and focus in order to start composing the new ballet in earnest. But, clearly, his mind was already full of ideas and he could not wait to get to Switzerland. A week before leaving Ustilug, he wrote to Roerich:

> I've already begun to compose and have sketched the Introduction for *dudki* [reed pipes], and the 'Divination with Twigs' in a state of passion and excitement. The music is coming out very fresh and new. The picture of the old woman in a squirrel fur sticks in my mind. She is constantly before my eyes as I compose the 'Divination with Twigs': I see her running in front of the group, stopping them sometimes, and interrupting the rhythmic flow.[19]

overleaf
Stravinsky at his composing desk.

In this letter, in which we see Stravinsky already deep into work on the first two sections of the work, we hear the first intimation that he felt that he was on to something very new with *The Rite of Spring*. We also see the extent to which the scenario agreed with Roerich was guiding, in detail, the music that he was writing. In later life, Stravinsky tried to distance himself from any plot or scenario in *The Rite*. Even as early as October 1912, he said to a journalist that it was not a ballet but 'simply a fantasia in two parts, like two movements of a symphony'[20] – so before he had even finished the piece, Stravinsky was casting his astute business eye towards its future life in the concert hall. But it is clear from what he said to his friends and collaborators at the time, as well as from looking at his sketches for *The Rite*, that the starting point for his explosive music was the set of prehistoric images, ancient rituals and mythic characters plotted out with Roerich at Talashkino.

In early October 1911, with the first notes of *The Rite of Spring* already committed to paper, the Stravinsky family took up residence at the modest guest house Les Tilleuls (The Lindens) overlooking Lake Geneva. The family was housed in a first-floor apartment that they quickly made their own. Stravinsky's biographer Stephen Walsh relates how the Stravinskys, who were perpetually on the move, 'had the habit of transforming their pension apartments into fragments of Bourgeois Russia, with hangings and drapes, prints, ornaments, clocks, family photographs and even small items of furniture'. Stravinsky's son Theodore later described this approach, which was to serve Stravinsky well in later life through the displacements he suffered because of revolution and war: 'Every time that we moved house for a few weeks my father always managed to give an air of permanence to what was in fact very temporary. . . All his life, wherever he might be, he always surrounded himself with his own atmosphere.'[21]

His own atmosphere extended to his work room. In a 1965 CBS documentary film, the eighty-two-year-old Stravinsky revisited Les Tilleuls with a camera crew, and proudly opened the door to the room 'in which I composed *Le Sacre du printemps*'.[22] The composing room was underneath the family apartment, rented separately as the work space in which he was to write his new ballet. The room was small – Stravinsky described it later as 'an eight-feet-by-eight closet. . . whose only furniture was a small upright piano which I kept muted, a table, and two chairs'. Stravinsky's composing table, wherever he went, was the same. A friend and future collaborator, Charles-Ferdinand Ramuz, compared the typical Stravinsky work table to that of a surgeon: a carefully ordered procession of bottles of differently coloured inks, a row of rubbers arranged according to their types and sizes, a glistening arrangement of metal implements: rulers, razors, knives and – an instrument of Stravinsky's own invention – a small contraption with tiny wheels designed to draw the five parallel lines of the music stave. In a photograph of one of his composing desks from around that time, the surgical look is softened by some family photographs and a vase of flowers.

The piano was also a permanent fixture of Stravinsky's composing rooms for all his life. If some composers write straight on to the paper, going to the piano only to check details, Stravinsky worked out his music from the very outset by finding the sounds and rhythms on the keyboard and only then writing it down. 'I need to feel the physicality of the music,' he later said in a television interview – and where more so than while he was composing a ballet in which he was trying find the ancient rhythms of the earth?

Stravinsky's deadline was to have the piece ready for performance at the end of the Ballets Russes' Paris season in late May of 1912. Throughout the winter of 1911 and into the spring of 1912, he worked in the small room in Clarens with a speed and intensity

overleaf
Sketches for *The Rite of Spring*, 1912, in which Stravinsky
announces that he has finished *Le Sacre* 'with a terrible toothache'.

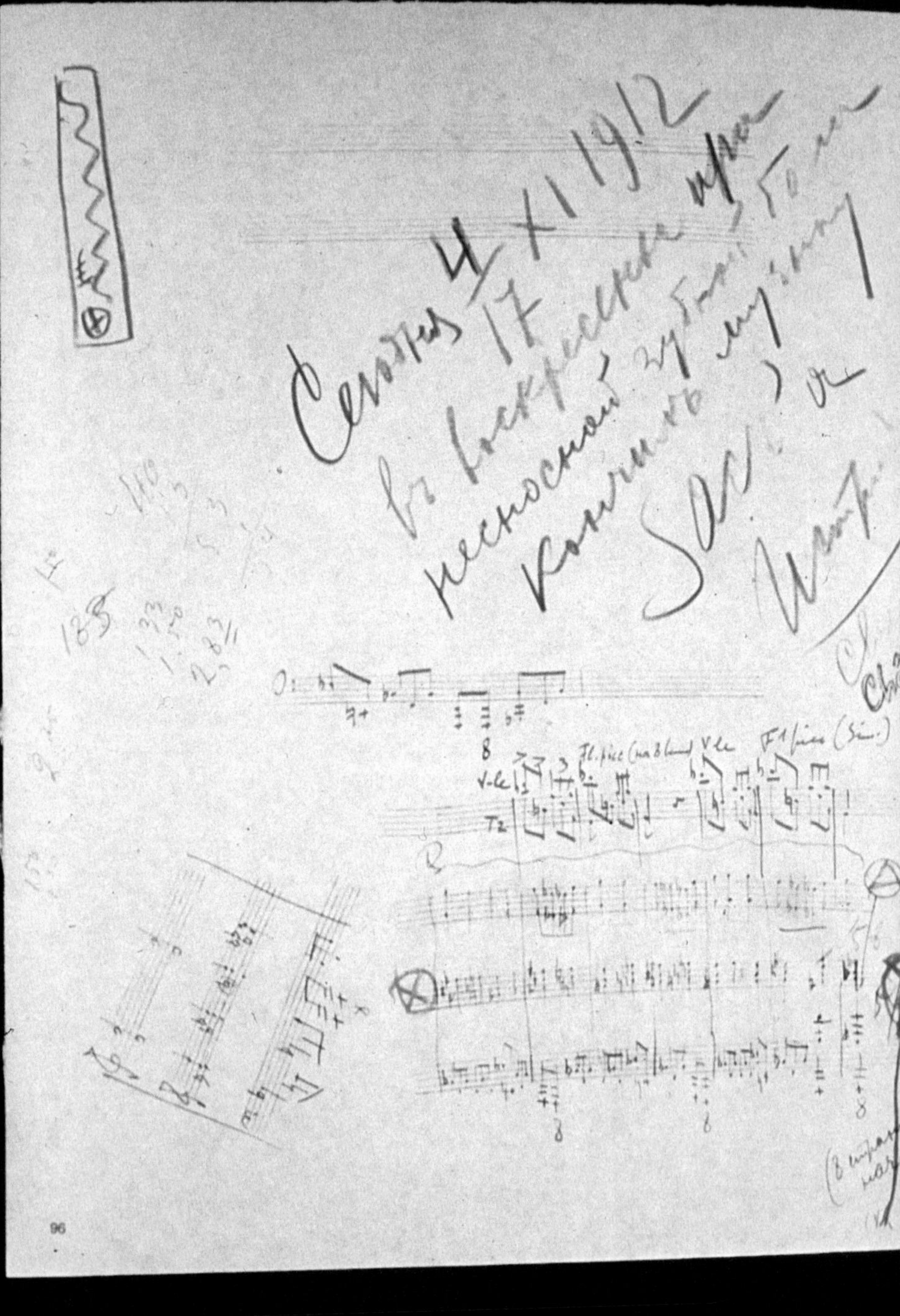
Сегодня 4 XI 1912

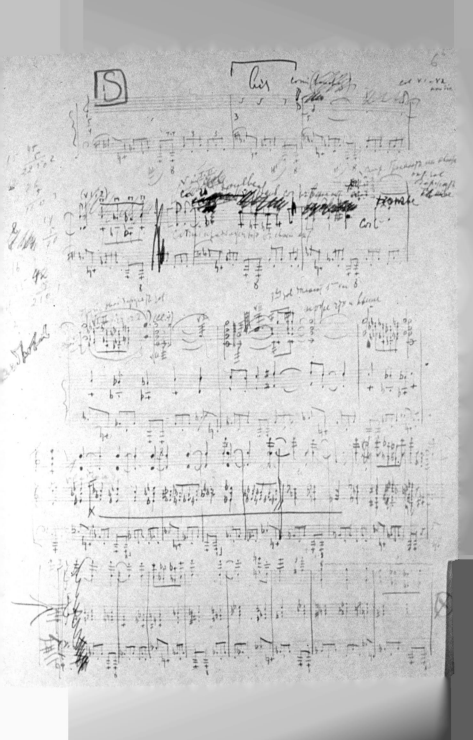

to which he and others have attributed near-miraculous status. Something, but not everything, about the process is revealed by looking at a notebook that Stravinsky filled with sketches for *The Rite of Spring*. The notepaper is plain, and Stravinsky has used his stave-drawing contraption to create only those staves he needs for the fragments of music he wanted to remember. The fragments are detached from each other and the appearance on the page is like floating islands or blocks that could be cut out and moved around. Sometimes these fragments consist of just a single musical gesture – a thumbnail sketch of a chord sequence, a melody line, a rhythm pattern; sometimes a whole page is filled up with an extended passage of full orchestral score. The sketches are neat and detailed and Stravinsky uses coloured inks and pencils to codify them: two different types of black ink are used as well as green and red. Throughout the sketches we see notes in Russian that remind us of the dramatic scenario he had agreed at Talashkino with Roerich: 'The Tribes', 'Action of the Ancestors', or 'Here, the Sacrificial Dance begins'; some of these titles are lightly sketched in pencil; one of them is ceremoniously spelled out at the top of a page in calligraphic, black-inked Cyrillic script. At one point, a huge arrow in thick blue pencil indicates that one block of music should move from one position on the page to another. There are scribbled practical notes to himself, also in Russian: 'Don't forget to put the woodwinds in octaves', or, more momentously, 'The End of *Le Sacre*' tucked away on the edge of one of the pages as a tiny pencil note next to a fragment of music depicting an orchestral flourish.

Although that particular orchestral flourish underwent several changes before its appearance as the final sound of *The Rite of Spring*, it is remarkable how vividly and recognizably the music of the finished work shines out from the broken-up shards of music in the sketchbook. On the very first page we see the unmistakable outline of the crunchy, dissonant chord that pounds through

'The Auguries of Spring', the first dance in the ballet, together with a fully worked-out representation of its irregular stamping rhythm. In a separate fragment, Stravinsky has written out the folk-like melody that will eventually go on top of it. In other tiny fragments of music drawn elsewhere on the page, we see ideas for elaborating the harmony, rhythm and melody of this section, all of which made the final cut of the piece. Over in one corner of the page, in red ink, is a tiny sketch indicating an idea for the choice of instruments Stravinsky might eventually make for this point in the music. These are not the laboured early workings of a tortured process, such as we see in Beethoven's sketches, but rather a set of remarkably complete musical objects, building blocks ready to be ordered, assembled and orchestrated to make the finished work. This sketchbook has gone some way to feed the story that the composition of *The Rite of Spring* was some kind of miracle, that it came to Stravinsky fully formed, from nothing, out of the air, in a dream. The more likely explanation is that all the detailed, laborious working out of his musical miracle was done as Stravinsky pounded away on the muted piano in the Swiss guest house: perspiration as well as inspiration.

In mid-November 1911, after six weeks or so of intense work in Clarens, Stravinsky travelled to Paris for a few days of recuperation. When Diaghilev got wind of the trip, he himself travelled to Paris from London and suggested a playthrough of what had so far been produced of the new ballet. This was the first of many carefully choreographed sneak previews of the work as Diaghilev, the deft publicist, built anticipation and buzz around *The Rite of Spring*. So, at the Paris salon of the Ballets Russes patroness Misia Edwards, Stravinsky played what he had written to Diaghilev and a small group that included the composers Maurice Ravel, Maurice Delage and Florent Schmitt. 'Everyone like it tremendously,' he wrote to Benois when he got back to Clarens.

No doubt encouraged by the positive response in Paris,

Stravinsky's speed of work seemed to increase as he worked through the winter and into the spring with the aim of finishing the first half of the ballet. On 6 March 1912, he was able to write to Roerich:

> A couple of words about our child. A week ago I completely finished the first tableau, meaning not only the music, but the orchestral score as well. Although the two plots are about equal in duration, the first tableau makes up a good three-quarters of the whole affair as far as the workload is concerned, because it consists entirely of madcap tempos and thus involves a lot of paperwork. I think the secret of the terse Spring rhythms was revealed to me, and I felt them in deep empathy with the protagonists of our child.[23]

In fact, by the time Stravinsky wrote this letter, he was already well into composing the second half of the ballet, and fully aware that this piece marked a huge leap forward for him. The day after the Roerich letter, he wrote to his friend Andrey Rimsky-Korsakov: 'My God, what a delight it will be to hear it. . . It's as if not two but twenty years have passed since I wrote *The Firebird*.'[24]

Meanwhile, the Ballets Russes company had arrived in Monte Carlo to rehearse for the 1912 season. Diaghilev, eager for an update on the new ballet, sent for Stravinsky, who interrupted his work to make the train journey from Lake Geneva to the Mediterranean. There the composer learned that the staging of *The Rite of Spring* was to be delayed until the following season. He also played through all the music he had so far completed in front of Diaghilev and Nijinsky. He wrote to his mother that both had liked it tremendously but also confessed in a letter to Benois, 'Seryozha [Diaghilev] was quite baffled by my sacred inspirations. It's something I was born with!'

It's significant that Diaghilev had invited Nijinsky and not Fokine to hear the playthrough of the new work. Fokine was the Ballets Russes' principal choreographer, who, it had always been intended, was going to stage *The Rite of Spring*. But despite the great success of Fokine's stagings of *The Firebird* and *Petrushka*, Stravinsky had become weary of his work and believed that he would not be up to the innovation this new kind of music demanded. Nijinsky, who was by that time Diaghilev's lover, was in the midst of rehearsals for his choreographic debut with the company, *L'Après-midi d'un faune*. All Diaghilev's instincts would have told him that *Faune* was going to be a *succès de scandale*, and it soon appeared inevitable that it was to be Nijinsky and not Fokine who would stage the new Stravinsky work. The subsequent rift with Fokine was bitter, and he resigned from the company in June that year.

A month later, Stravinsky was back in Monte Carlo, where he was able to play the music of *The Rite* to the final member of the artistic team, Pierre Monteux, who was to conduct the first performances. Monteux's first reaction to hearing the music has become part of the mythology of *The Rite of Spring*.

> With only Diaghilev and myself as audience, Stravinsky sat down to play a piano reduction of the entire [sic] score. Before he got very far I was convinced he was raving mad. Heard this way, without the colour of the orchestra, which is one of its greatest distinctions, the crudity of the rhythm was emphasized, its stark primitiveness underlined. The very walls resounded as Stravinsky pounded away, occasionally stamping his feet and jumping up and down to accentuate the force of the music.[25]

Relieved of the immediate pressure of a 1912 deadline and with a significant chunk of *The Rite of Spring* already under his belt, Stravinsky could afford to follow the Ballets Russes company to Paris. There he attended the premiere of *L'Après-midi d'un faune* – Diaghilev got the scandal he had anticipated – and, a few days later, Stravinsky played what he had completed of *The Rite* to a group of friends including the composer of *L'Après-midi*, Claude Debussy. Debussy later wrote, 'I still preserve the memory of the performance of your *Sacre du printemps* at Laloy's. . . It haunts me like a beautiful nightmare and I try in vain to retrieve the terrifying impression it made. For which reason I look forward to its production like a greedy child who has been promised sweets.'[26] Despite this rather qualified praise, Debussy always had an uneasy relationship with *The Rite of Spring*, quipping privately that it was 'primitive music with all modern conveniences'.[27]

In June, Stravinsky returned to his home in Ustilug where he worked hard on *The Rite*, but, ever restless, he was soon on the move again: an August trip to the Wagner Festival in Bayreuth to meet Diaghilev and see a performance of *Parsifal* and, in early October, his last visit for half a century to his home city of St Petersburg. In late October, he moved the family back to Clarens for the winter, this time to the Hôtel du Châtelard. Finally, one month after arriving back in Switzerland, Stravinsky wrote in the sketchbook, in large letters in a combination of blue and red pencil: 'Today 4/17 November 1912, Sunday, with an unbearable toothache, I finished the music of the *Sacre*. I. Strav. Clarens, Châtelard Hotel.' There was still work to do on orchestration, which he got down to in the ensuing days while on a train to attend the Ballets Russes performances of *The Firebird* and *Petrushka*. But, essentially, the music of *The Rite of Spring* was complete.

Stravinsky was frustrated that he had to leave Berlin before Nijinsky started rehearsals with the dancers for *The Rite*, but he was cheered to find, when he got back to Clarens, that Roerich had sent him the finished costume designs, worked up from the original Talashkino ideas and wrote straight back: 'I am pleased that they were sent to me first so that I could see them – they are a real miracle, and I only hope that the realization of them will be good.' Hinting that he knew the scale of the challenge that the inexperienced Nijinsky had in front of him, he added, 'How I hope that Nijinsky has time enough to stage the *Spring*. It is very complex, and I feel that it must be done as nothing has ever been done before!'[28]

Diaghilev realized that Nijinsky would, indeed, need help in grasping the unprecedented complexity of Stravinsky's music. He had heard about the work of Émile Jaques-Dalcroze, the Swiss composer and music educator whose Eurhythmics method aimed to teach the principles of music through physical movement. Believing that Eurhythmics might hold the key to the new kind of choreography that Stravinsky's music demanded, Diaghilev took Nijinsky on a visit to Dalcroze's headquarters in the progressive artistic community in the garden city of Hellerau near Dresden. The twenty-four-year-old Polish dancer and musician Myriam Ramberg, one of Dalcroze's assistants, described how the elegantly dressed Russian pair made an impression as they stood watching a class, Diaghilev with his leisurely, aristocratic bearing and Nijinsky with his pale complexion and light brown eyes, 'slit slightly upward'.[29] The next day, to her astonishment, Ramberg was summoned to meet Diaghilev who, on the advice of Dalcroze, invited her to join the Ballets Russes company on tour for some 'special work'. Ramberg joined the company in Budapest and,

Marie Rambert, future founder of the Ballet Rambert, photographed in 1925.

with her advanced musical training and dance knowledge, soon became indispensable to the rehearsal process for the new ballet. It was around this time that she changed her name to Marie Rambert, under which name, much later in her life, she was to be an enormously influential figure in modern dance in the United Kingdom.

The company was touring all over Europe – Berlin, Budapest, Vienna, Wrocław, Leipzig, Monte Carlo – and rehearsals for the new work were fitted around the performance schedule, with only a few days in each city. Nijinsky, who was dancing principal roles in the company's repertoire as well as preparing *The Rite* and his new Debussy ballet *Jeux*, was feeling the strain. But, even under stress, he did not lose sight of the idea that this ballet was something new and momentous. On 25 January 1913, he wrote to Stravinsky from Leipzig to report good progress in rehearsal: 'If the work continues like this, Igor, the result will be something great.'[30]

But there were tensions in the rehearsal room, with many of the dancers hostile to Nijinsky's approach. Sergey Grigoriev, the company's ballet master, was an ally of the deposed Fokine and did little to support Nijinsky. '[The dancers] saw little point in Nijinsky's composition, which consisted almost entirely of rhythmical stamping without any other movement. It was my delicate duty to settle differences and keep the peace between the choreographer and the company; and I did my best to maintain morale by rehearsing some of the old Fokine ballets by way of relief.'[31] Marie Rambert was firmly on Nijinsky's side, and believed that his vision for *The Rite* was utterly original and thrilling, but she admits that his working methods exasperated and exhausted the dancers. Fokine's dance had allowed fluidity and spontaneity between the balletic gestures, but Nijinsky wanted to control every single movement; there was a step for each note of the piece, every element of the dancer's body was prescribed at all times.

This approach meant that the pace of rehearsals was glacially slow. And, to slow things up even more, Nijinsky was a poor communicator. Words did not come easily to him and, Rambert remembers, he taught the dancers the steps by demonstrating everything himself. The steps themselves were simple – walking or stamping, jumping, mostly off both feet and landing heavily – but everything had to be done from a basic stance, which, the dancers complained, was awkward and the exact opposite of their classical training: feet were turned in instead of out, knees bent, arms in the opposite of the classical position. The impression was of heavy, earthbound movement rather than gravity-defying airborne lightness. All this was designed to create what Rambert described as 'a primitive, prehistoric posture'[32] but it seemed to Nijinsky's ballet artists that it was a kind of anti-dance.

The biggest stress on the company, however, came from the newness and complexity of Stravinsky's music. Grigoriev remembered that the dancers complained that rehearsals were more like arithmetic classes, with the main business being the counting of the constantly changing metres as the music was pounded out on a piano by a fat German pianist Diaghilev had nicknamed 'Kolossal'. 'Some of the girls used to be running around with little bits of paper in their hands, in a panic, quarrelling with each other about whose count was right and whose wrong,' remembered the English dancer Hilda Munnings, who joined the company for the first time during the *Rite* rehearsals in Monte Carlo and was known thereafter as Lydia Sokolova.[33] Marie Rambert's main job was to make sure that both Nijinsky and the dancers learned the rhythms – the company soon gave her the nickname Rhythmichka – and she coached each artist individually as well as meeting Nijinsky every evening after rehearsal to go through the music for the next day.

By all accounts, when Stravinsky visited Nijinsky's rehearsals, he did nothing to build his confidence. Rambert describes one visit where he pushed Kolossal off the piano stool and started to play the music himself, twice as fast as Nijinsky had been rehearsing it, stamping his feet, banging his fist on the piano, singing and shouting that *this* was how it should go. Stravinsky made no secret of the fact that he thought that the choreographer had a poor grasp of music. Nijinsky's sister, the principal dancer Bronislawa, reported a conversation with her brother:

> Bronia, I am often exasperated by Igor Fyodorovich. I have a great respect for him as a musician, and we have been friends for years, but so much time is wasted as Stravinsky thinks he is the only one who knows anything about music. In working with me he explains the value of the black notes, the white notes, of quavers and semiquavers, as though I had never studied music at all.[34]

But even the loyal Bronia was soon to add to Nijinsky's woes. He had intended that she dance the role of the sacrificial victim, the Chosen One, the only significant solo in the ballet, but once the company reached Monte Carlo, she had to tell her brother that she was pregnant and would have to pull out. 'You are deliberately trying to destroy my work, just like all the others!' was his response.[35]

When Grigoriev told Diaghilev of the difficulties in the rehearsal room, he allegedly replied, true to form, 'An excellent sign!'[36] But it was clear that he needed to find the company some time to work through the problems, free from the obligations of touring and performing. Thanks to the patronage of businessman Sir Joseph Beecham, heir to the powders and pills empire, theatre owner and father of the conductor Thomas Beecham, the company settled in at the Aldwych Theatre for six weeks of uninterrupted rehearsal between February and March. It was here, in London's West End, that *The Rite of Spring* finally began to come together.

No one has been able to put a precise figure on the number of dance rehearsals that took place all round Europe between December 1912 and the premiere on 29 May 1913. 'Hundreds' is a word that appears in several of the accounts; Stravinsky estimated it at 130. What we do know is that the Paris orchestra, under Pierre Monteux, had seventeen full rehearsals, plus additional sessions with the individual orchestral sections (an orchestra today would, typically, have three full rehearsals for a thirty-minute new work). After the initial shock of the playthrough in Monte Carlo, Monteux appeared to be taking it all in his stride, writing to Stravinsky to report good progress and asking about technical questions related to bar numbers, instruments and mutes. But Henri Girard, a double-bass-player in the orchestra, remembered that the shock of the music was as great for the musicians as it had been for the dancers:

> Everybody was confused by the complicated rhythms, atrocious dissonances and strange sounds to which our ears were not accustomed. Musicians started to stop Monteux, asking if the parts were correctly printed, wanting to know for example, if 'my B natural is correct as my neighbour is playing B flat'.[37]

When the Ballets Russes company arrived in early May, the close artistic world of Paris to which they belonged was in shock. The children of Isadora Duncan had been drowned with their nanny when the car that they were travelling in had rolled into the Seine. Ravel wrote to Stravinsky: 'Tomorrow I go to see that unfortunate Isadora Duncan. I tremble at the thought. It is really too awful, too unjust.'[38]

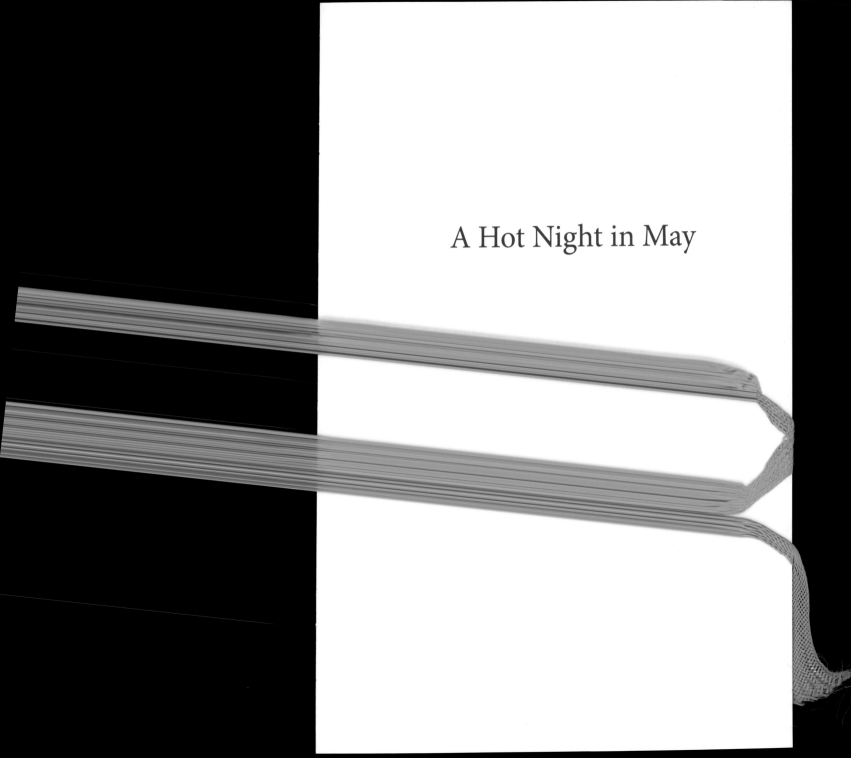

A Hot Night in May

'So where on earth were these bastards brought up?' was not, perhaps, a sentence the elite of Paris expected to read about themselves on the front page of a leading cultural journal. But that's what the editor of *Comœdia*, Gaston de Pawlowski, wrote on 31 May 1913, about the audience at the riotous premiere of *Le Sacre du printemps* given by the Ballets Russes two days earlier at the brand-new Théâtre des Champs-Élysées. Pawlowski's 'bastards' covered a relatively wide social range. Under the term, he included the beau monde: the old money of the aristocrats and the new money of the industrialists and financiers, the wealthy patronesses of the arts who had swept into the Théâtre des Champs-Élysées on 29 May with their jewels, turbans and feathers. He also included the aesthetes: the intellectuals, artists – some famous – and students who had crowded the cheaper seats and the gangways. Pawlowski did not reserve his bile for the 'stupid and intentional nastiness' of those who were predisposed to hate Stravinsky's, Nijinsky's and Roerich's new ballet. In the sabotage of the premiere, he insisted, *The Rite of Spring*'s fans were equally to blame: 'It was only by cupping our ears in the middle of an indescribable racket that we could painfully grasp an approximate idea of this new work, which was drowned out equally by its defenders and its adversaries,' he continued. 'This was not *Le Sacre* but *Le Massacre du Printemps*.'

The first performance of *The Rite of Spring* is one of the most famous events in the history of art – and one of the most contested. The two big stories from that night were the shock of a ballet that, to its fans and its foes alike, seemed to have arrived from nowhere and the bad behaviour of the audience. Journalists could not get enough of the story, and there are over a hundred accounts and reviews of the event in the newspapers and magazines of the time. It is described in memoirs written and anecdotes recounted by the major personalities who created the work. Then there are the stories told by some of the ballet's more than two hundred dancers and musicians who wrote or talked about their experiences at the time or years later, and there are memories, polemics, one-liners and considered analyses from some of the well-known artistic personalities in the audience. From these accounts, we can conjure up a picture of the night of 29 May at the Théâtre des Champs-Élysées from many different viewpoints: from on the stage, from the orchestra pit, from different seats in the theatre, from the wings, from backstage, from the foyer. And yet this most notorious of first nights is still, to a large extent, unknowable. Many of the stories contradict each other, shrouding the events of the night in a mist of uncertainty. It is difficult, for example, to pin down reliably who was in the audience and who was not. And what, exactly, caused the riot itself? Was it the music? Or the dancing? And were the police really called to the theatre? Has the whole thing been exaggerated

Champs-Élysées

among Parisian audiences. It had opened its doors for the first time just eight weeks earlier, the visionary project of concert promoter Gabriel Astruc. Astruc was a colourful force on the city's arts scene. As well as working as agent for artists as diverse as the exotic dancer and future spy Mata Hari and the Russian

he had created the Grande Saison de

and contemporary spice after the

of the autumn–winter artistic season in Paris was over. Sergey Diaghilev's Ballets Russes had been, since 1909, the exotic jewel in the crown of Astruc's season. Naturally, the company was to have a major presence in the new theatre's opening weeks. On 6 May, *Comœdia* announced:

overleaf
Part of Antoine Bourdelle's marble frieze on the exterior of the Théâtre des Champs-Élysées.

Our Friends the Russians Are Back! This hails the most significant season yet of the lyrical, choreographic and decorative sides of Slavic art which has won so many admirers among us. . . Igor Stravinsky will complete his trilogy of balletic works with the most striking of all, *Le Sacre du printemps*, in which all the features, the technical, choreographic, choral and orchestral composition and the visual presentation will be subjects of interest and astonishment.

The hype was critical for Astruc as he had invested heavily in the 1913 spring season. Diaghilev had seen the monetary value of the craze for the Ballets Russes and had negotiated double the previous fee. Astruc needed a sell-out.

The position of the new theatre on the Avenue Montaigne, just off the Champs-Élysées, was part of a push to shift the cultural axis of the French capital towards the more fashionable western part of the city. But its architecture was also a cultural statement in itself. Designed by Auguste Perret, it was the first public building in Paris to be built of reinforced concrete, which was wrapped in plain white marble. Its simple, unadorned lines appeared austere and arrestingly modern, in stark contrast to the imperial opulence of the nineteenth-century Opéra Garnier and the Châtelet theatres further east. Yes, there was some decoration – an exterior frieze by sculptor Antoine Bourdelle and a domed ceiling painted by Maurice Denis – but these were classical and restrained, and did not obscure the hard, clean lines of the architecture. Whereas at the old Opéra Garnier, loges des scènes (stage boxes) thrust out into the sightlines to the stage so that the richest people could be seen by everyone in the house, Astruc's new theatre had a more democratic ambience, with the boxes placed behind the ordinary seating and a close connection between the cheaper and the more expensive seats – something that was to prove fateful on 29 May. As the painter Jacques-Émile Blanche, who was in the audience that night, put it:

The gamble undertaken by the founders of the Théâtre des Champs-Élysées involved what they thought they could do to bring together in an artistic milieu those who go to a spectacle to be seen or to take medicinal pleasure, and those who go there to be renewed. They wanted to instil in the first type the spiritual outlook of the second.

The new stage was designed as a simple square in a plain frame, creating a sense of isolation and distance from the audience, like the screen in the newest art form, cinema. The Champs-Élysées was to be the ideal theatre for the modern age and all the focus was to be on the art. Jacques-Émile Blanche again:

> … the foyer you felt there a sense
>
> of Bunnelmonty…
> we wanted to play classic works and welcome …
> departures.[1]

The reference to Wagner's Festival Theatre is telling. One of the most bitter criticisms of the new theatre was that the architecture was 'too German'. Peter Behrens had recently built his pioneering concrete Turbine Factory in Berlin, and Adolf … urging a new simplicity in arch… year. The idea that there was an Austro-Ger… the new theatre did not go down well in the Paris of 1913 against a backdrop of mounting international tension and a ferocious arms race.

The twenty-ninth of May 1913 was a hot day in Paris, and a heatwave was predicted, with some light rain forecast for about ten in the evening. That morning, the following announcement appeared in a number of newspapers:

> *The Rite of Spring*, which the Russian Ballet will perform for the first time this evening at the Théâtre des Champs-Élysées, is the most amazing creation ever attempted by M. Serge de Diaghilev's admirable company. It evokes the primitive gestures of pagan Russia as conceived by the triple vision of Stravinsky, poet and composer, of Nicholas Roerich, poet and painter, and of Nijinsky, poet and choreographer.

Here we see powerfully portrayed the characteristic attitudes of the Slavic race in its response to beauty in the prehistoric era.

> Only the wonderful Russian dancers could portray these first stammered gestures of half-savage humanity; only they could represent these frenzied mobs of people who stamp out untiringly the most startling polyrhythms ever produced by the brain of a musician. Here is truly a new sensation which will undoubtedly provoke heated discussions, but will leave every spectator with an unforgettable memory of the artists.[2]

This press release was written by Astruc but it had the hand of Diaghilev, the instinctive publicist, all over it. It shows that Astruc and Diaghilev were anticipating or perhaps even actively seeking a scandal. It also makes it clear that they wanted the ballet to be received as a truly collaborative, total work of art, the combined vision of three artists of equal importance: the thirty-one-year-old composer Igor Stravinsky, unheard of in Paris or pretty much anywhere until three years previously, but whose reputation as a prodigiously gifted composer rested solely on two spectacularly successful ballet scores: *The Firebird* and *Petrushka*, written for Diaghilev's 1910 and 1912 Paris seasons respectively; the Ballet Russes star dancer Vaslav Nijinsky, hailed as a god of the dance, Diaghilev's lover, but regarded with suspicion as a choreographer since the critical failure of his versions of Debussy's *L'Après-midi d'un faune* and *Jeux*, and Nicholas Roerich, painter, set-designer, and the strongest contender as the intellectual guru behind the Russian one.

Also on the morning of 29 May, an article appeared in the avant-garde cultural magazine *Montjoie!* in which Stravinsky outlined the scenario for the new ballet, and warned readers that it was going to be something very new, with neither the fairy tales of *The Firebird* nor the simple human sadness and joy of *Petrushka*. *The Rite of Spring* was to be about something more elemental: 'In *The Rite of Spring*, I have desired to express the sublime growth of nature which renews itself: the total Panic ascent of the universal sap.'

Stravinsky later denied having written the article, condemning it as 'naive', but it all fed the publicity machine, as had the open rehearsals in the days leading up to the premiere, to which Diaghilev had invited a carefully selected private audience of musicians, writers and critics. Some, including the composer and conductor Louis Vuillemin writing in *Comœdia*, suggested that these rehearsals were designed to whip up feelings and draw the battle lines for the riotous premiere in advance:

> Some people, invited to a few final rehearsals, went back out
> into the streets of Paris wild-looking and convinced they had
> reason to be. They were of two kinds: both wild and both
> convinced. 'Marvellous, magnificent, splendid, definitive!' cried
> some to everyone who would listen for a moment. 'Abominable,
> hateful, ridiculous, pretentious!' screamed the others even to
> those who did not have time to listen. I leave it to you to
> surmise the kind of damage brought about by such passion. It
> spread through the entire public like wildfire thirty-six hours
> before the curtain rose. 'Just you wait,' those convinced said. 'We
> are about to witness the great musical revolution. This evening
> is the appointed time for the symphony of the future!' 'Watch
> out!' warned the sceptics. 'They are out to make fun of us. They
> take us for fools. We must defend ourselves!'

The weather remained hot into the evening as the audience arrived at the Avenue Montaigne for the performance, scheduled to start at 8.45 p.m. Although the advance publicity left no doubt in anybody's mind as to what the main event was, *The Rite of Spring* had been programmed as part of a generous sandwich of familiar and popular Ballets Russes fare. It was to be embedded in an inviting sequence of three ballets choreographed by Michel Fokine, until 1912 the popular chief choreographer of the Ballets Russes, until Diaghilev sacked him and put Nijinsky in his place. The Fokine ballets were set to familiar and palatable music: *Les Sylphides* was a 'Romantic Reverie' with music by Chopin; *Le Spectre de la rose* had music by Weber, and *Polovtsian Dances* used extracts from Borodin's tuneful opera *Prince Igor*. *The Rite of Spring* would be performed, after an interval, between *Les Sylphides* and *Le Spectre de la rose*. *Sylphides* and *Spectre* starred Nijinsky as a dancer, a fact that might have been designed to compensate the audience for his lack of appearance in *The Rite of Spring*, which was to be, with the exception of the final dance of the sacrificial victim, a ballet without soloists.

A significant number of the well-to-do faction of the audience would have rolled up at the front door in motorcars, and the programme book they picked up at the door, set in a highly contemporary art deco typeface, contained advertisements for Peugeot, Renault and Mercedes Benz. Those of the women who were up to date with contemporary style would, with their dresses and head-gear, have looked as though they belonged on stage with the Ballets Russes. Alongside the wealthy elite and the affluent bohemian types who attended that night were artists, musicians and students heading for the cheap seats. Jean Cocteau observed the different groups who came through the doors of the Théâtre des Champs-Élysées with a cold and cynical gaze, predicting, with the benefit of hindsight, an explosive mix:

Drawing of Stravinsky rehearsing *The Rite of Spring*, by Jean Cocteau.

All the elements of a scandal were present. The ...
... tails and tulle, diamonds and ospreys was interspersed with
... ... crowd. The latter would

the boxes. Innumerable ...
inverted snobbery were represented which would need a chapter
to themselves. . . The audience played the role that was written
for it.[3]

Cocteau was one of a significant number of artistic celebrities
in the packed theatre. The roll-call of famous names in attendance
on the evening of 29 May has been a matter of speculation for
more than a century. We know for certain that the composers
Ravel, Debussy, Delius, Florent Schmitt and Alfredo Casella
were in the house. Puccini is often said to have been there, but
the documents show that he went to the second performance,
declaring, 'The choreography is ridiculous, the music sheer

cacophony. . . taken together, it might be the work of a madman.'[4] Gertrude Stein implied that she had been at the riotous first performance: 'We could hear nothing. . . One literally could not, throughout the whole performance, hear the sound of the music.'[5] But in *The Autobiography of Alice B. Toklas* Stein makes it clear that, like Puccini, she and Toklas had attended not the first but the second performance, an altogether quieter affair.[6] A twenty-first-century film about the first night of *The Rite of Spring* places Pablo Picasso in the stalls, furiously sketching throughout the performance. Picasso's future wife Olga Khokhlova was one of the dancers on the stage – the pair were not to meet until 1917 – but Cocteau states categorically that Picasso was not in the theatre that night. We do know, however, that the seventy-seven-year-old Mélanie, Comtesse de Pourtalès, whose salons had been renowned since the the days of the Second Empire, was there: several witnesses report her crying out, after the end of the new ballet, 'This is the first time in sixty years that anyone has dared make fun of me!' Cocteau adds the detail that her face was red and her tiara askew, compounding the sense of affront to the old world.[7] A patron of the arts of the younger generation, Misia Edwards (later Sert), a sponsor of the Ballets Russes, was also present and was spellbound by the ballet. Claude Debussy, however, who was seated next to her in her box, had a more distressing experience. As Edwards leaned over to him to share her wonder at the new work, she noted that 'A terrible sadness was reflected on his anxious face. He bent over me and whispered: "It is horrible – I can hear nothing."'[8]

On returning to their seats in the hot theatre after *Les Sylphides*, the audience would have opened their programme books to read about what to expect for the next half-hour. The synopsis printed there read as follows:

First Act: The Adoration of the Earth. Spring; the earth is covered with flowers. The earth is covered with grass. A great joy reigns on the earth. The men begin to dance and question the future according to the rites. The Ancestor of all the Sages takes part himself in the Glorification of Spring. He is brought out to be united with the abundant and great earth. Everyone stamps the earth in ecstasy.

Second Act: The Sacrifice. After nightfall; after midnight. On the hills there are sacred stones. The young girls play mystical games and seek the Grand Way. They glorify the one who has been chosen to be offered up to God. They call up the Ancestors as venerable witnesses. And the wise Ancestors of the men watch the Sacrifice. It is thus that they sacrifice to Yarilo the magnificent, the flaming.

The lights went down and the audience fell silent. The curtain remained closed, which it would for the entire three-minute 'Introduction' with which the ballet began. A strange, lonely, reedy sound floated up from the orchestra pit, casting a sinuous, improvisatory line out into the theatre. This weird melody was soon joined by other wind instruments creeping and sliding around in a kind of primeval mud out of which the stirrings, buzzings and calls of spring started to emerge and multiply and grow into a dense, rhythmically free collage of nature sounds. The critic Georges Pioch wrote the next day that a small controversy arose in the seats around him about what that opening reedy sound was: was it an oboe? a muted trumpet? a clarinet? He was astonished to learn later from the conductor that it was a bassoon, playing higher than had previously been thought possible or, at least, tasteful. The audience shifted in their seats. The conductor Pierre Monteux (who had been instructed by Diaghilev to keep going, whatever happened) remembered afterwards, 'The audience remained quiet for the first two minutes. Then came boos and catcalls from the gallery, soon after from the lower

overleaf
Male dancers in *The Rite*, dressed in heavy tunics and fur hats. On seeing their jerking, knock-kneed movements, a section of the audience – in Cocteau's words – 'immediately rebelled'.

5 дейст.

Б. Геннл Нарыгь.

degenerated into a public meeting', with insults and opinions being thrown around the auditorium.[16] Several reports say that an elegant lady hissed, 'Sale Juif!' ('Dirty Jew!') at Ravel, who was not, as it happens, Jewish.[17] Astruc, however, was. Only seven years after the end of the Dreyfus affair, which had laid bare the anti-Semitism of the French establishment, such undercurrents were still not far beneath the surface. The artist Valentine Gross-Hugo, who provided invaluable sketches of the dance rehearsals for *The Rite*, reported the rage of Stravinsky's composer friends:

> Delage, garnet red with indignation; Maurice Ravel aggressive as a small fighting cock; [Léon-Paul] Fargue, roaring vengeful epithets towards the hissing boxes. I was amazed that this work, so difficult for 1913, could be played and danced to the very end in such an uproar.[18]

Indeed, through the storm Monteux kept conducting, the orchestra kept playing and the dancers kept dancing, but the racket from the auditorium meant that the dancers could not hear the music on the stage. Lydia Sokolova wrote:

> We were all terrified that we were doing the fourth, fifth or sixth steps, while somebody else was doing the second; and Nijinsky was in the wings stamping and trying to count for different groups all at once. We could see Diaghilev too, walking up and down, holding his head. We must have been a lovely picture for the audience, racing around, jumping, turning, and wondering when the whole thing was going to collapse.[19]

Stravinsky, meanwhile, was sitting in the theatre, a few rows back from the stage in the right-hand section of the stalls. Years later, he remembered that he spent his time in the theatre staring hard at Monteux's back, willing him to continue, amazed that the conductor appeared 'nerveless and impervious as a crocodile'[20] with all the noise going on around him. But as the clamour mounted, Stravinsky left his seat in distress and anger – in a later documentary film, he remembered saying 'Go to Hell!' to some protesting audience members as he pushed along the row to get out.[21] He almost certainly did not, as Pierre Monteux later claimed, sneak out of a back window and wander the streets of Paris in despair, but went backstage. There, he says, he found Nijinsky standing on a chair, just out of sight of the audience, shouting numbers to the dancers: 'I wondered what on earth these numbers had to do with the music for there are no "thirteens" and "seventeens" in the metrical scheme of the score.'[22]

Nijinsky had danced the lead role in *Les Sylphides* before the interval, and would return to the stage after *The Rite* for *Le Spectre de la rose*, so he was directing the dancing from the wings in his practice costume and make-up. Romola Pulszky described him beating out the rhythm with his fists for the dancers who could not hear the music over the din from the audience, shouting, 'Ras, dwa, tri,'* his face as white as his dancing shirt. Bronislawa Nijinska, Nijinsky's sister and another Ballets Russes star, was not dancing that night because of her pregnancy. But she stayed backstage to support her brother, and she described her concern for his well-being:

> I could see that Vaslav was in a state of extreme anxiety lest the artists got things wrong. He appeared on the point of rushing onstage to restore some kind of order in case the artists went to pieces. . . Standing in the wings I had felt weak and my legs had failed me. My heart was tight, not so much for the fate of the ballet as for Vaslav.[23]

From his box at the back of the theatre, Diaghilev shouted a number of times to the audience, 'Let them finish the performance!'[24] At some stage either he or Astruc decided that

---

* Transliteration of the Russian for 'One, two, three.'

turning the house lights on and off would help quieten things down but, if this had any effect, it was only temporary. Lydia Sokolova wrote that there was a crescendo in the protests towards the end of the first act of the ballet: 'The first scene ended with a burst of whistling from the front of the house, and we were extremely glad when the curtain came down. But we still had to change our costumes for Act Two, which was more difficult, if anything.' She was not the only person to remember whistling: the critic Victor Debay, in his review, noted, 'The Russian Dancers. . . suddenly found out that the elegant and aristocratic audiences which are their usual clientele have whistles in their pockets and know how to use them.'[25] Several witnesses remember that Astruc took to the stage between the two acts to appeal for calm, but none of the reviews reports this.

Part of the mythology that has grown up around the events of 29 May 1913 is that the police were called to restore order at the theatre. However, none of the contemporary accounts of the premier say that this was the case. Henri Girard, a double-bassist from the orchestra, expressly said that they were not. But several people writing long after the event mention a police presence. The ballet master Grigoriev said that Diaghilev had put the house lights on so that the police could pick out and eject some of the worst offenders before the second act. Monteux made similar claims – 'At last, the gendarmes arrived'[26] – as did the dancer Sokolova. But Grigoriev would have been backstage for the entire performance; Sokolova might have had other things on her mind as she tried to keep dancing, and Monteux and Girard were in the pit, so they are unlikely to have seen the police for themselves. In a tantalizing twist, the performance historian Esteban Buch points out in an article from 2013 that the police records for the district police station of the Champs-Élysées for the period between February 1913 and April 1914 have gone missing. We will never know for sure.[27]

Vaslav Nijinsky in *Le Spectre de la rose*, 1911.

By the halfway point of the ballet, the atmosphere in the Théâtre des Champs-Élysées was, by all accounts, at its most intense. At this point, it is worth pausing to look at what the audience had just experienced and examining why, after only fifteen minutes, it had whipped up such a frenzy of outrage.* The disconcerting effect of the strange new sounds in the 'Introduction' and the violent shock of the opening dance when the curtain rose was followed by a series of games and rituals: a game where young men play out the abduction of a bride, a slow *khorovod* performed by young girls, a mock battle between rival tribes, a procession of elders headed by the Sage who blesses the earth with a kiss and, finally, a violent 'Dance of the Earth'. There is none of the usual balletic soft edges or blurry transformations between these sections in either the music or in the dance. The different scenes are cut and spliced together like film; there is no connecting tissue. The music certainly delivered, as promised that morning in the press release, 'the most startling polyrhythms ever produced by the brain of a musician' but there was much more besides. There was a most original approach to dissonance, in which melody lines or chords in themselves familiar are combined with other similar melodies and chords. Each would be conventional on its own, but put together they create a dissonant crunch that is both alienating and familiar. And there was an approach to orchestration that, from the very first phrase on the bassoon, would have startled the audience. Another arresting effect would have been the music for the 'Procession of the Sage', where the repetitive scraping and banging of the percussion section in rhythmic counterpoint with the rest of the orchestra sounds like deafening industrial noise from an early twentieth-century motorcar factory. The audience might never have heard anything so loud from an orchestra.

---

* Readers might find it useful here to refer to Chapter 6, '*The Rite* Step by Step: A Listening Guide'.

The dance was no less innovative. The flat-footed, knock-kneed 'anti-ballet' shape into which Nijinsky moulded the bodies of his dancers went against their training and the audience's expectations. It was designed to create a sense of the 'other', a distancing alienation through which the audience could imagine an ancient people. Nijinsky, famous for his gravity-defying leaps, got his dancers jumping in *The Rite* – over and over again – but, as dance historian Millicent Hodson has pointed out, the jumps had a low centre of gravity and presented other challenges: 'The body is not straight up in the jumps but still has to rise vertically.'[28] Apart from the 'Sacrificial Dance (The Chosen One)' at the very end of the ballet, there were no solos – those traditional audience pleasers. The old Sorceress from the beginning and the Sage were the briefest of cameos. Hodson says that Nijinsky's *Rite* is a ballet about massed energy, about the movement of groups of people around the stage. It is a choral ballet, but not in the traditional sense of an ensemble moving in unison. Groups move together, spin round, move on the spot, split to form other groups, which then move in counterpoint with each other before splitting apart again. Within these teeming groups of people, individuals often seem lost in their own world, going round and round in their own particular repetitive, obsessive movement. The young critic Jacques Rivière, in a brilliantly perceptive essay written months after the premiere, described *The Rite of Spring* as 'a biological ballet', linking it to discoveries in science from recent decades:

> One would think he is witnessing a drama beneath a
> microscope; it is the story of Karyokinesis, the profound labour
> of the seed by which it separates and reproduces itself; the
> division of birth, scissions, and reunions of turbulent matter in
> its very substance; large turning masses of protoplasm,
> germinative slabs, zones, circles, placentae.[29]

It's not hard to see why all this was profoundly disturbing to an audience fed on the great Russian ballet tradition. The critic Pierre Lalo vehemently expressed the outrage of the choreographic traditionalists:

> Not one line, not one movement of one character offers the appearance of grace, of elegance of lightness of nobility or of expression; everything is ugly – heavily, flatly, uniformly ugly. The dancers, almost always squeezed into tight and compact groups, stay jammed together, making only clumsy, short, crabbed and constrained gestures, the motions of the crippled or the ataxic. They shake their arms as if they were stumps and their legs as if they were made of wood. They never dance; all they do is jump, paw the ground, stamp, and shake convulsively in place.

Lalo's review was more respectful of Stravinsky, putting faith in his track record with *The Firebird* and *Petrushka*, but he none the less expressed, in colourful terms, the kind of bafflement that the music must have induced in large sections of the audience:

> Its essential characteristic is that it is the most dissonant and discordant music yet composed. Never has the cult and practice of the wrong-note technique been practised with such industry, such zeal, or such determination. From the first bar of the work to the last, whatever note is anticipated, it is never that one that is heard but the one nearest it, the note which should not be expected; whatever the chord may be which seems to follow from the preceding chord, another is heard; and that very chord and that note are intentionally used to give the feeling of a bitter, almost excruciating disharmony. Whatever two themes are superimposed, far from taking themes that would 'go together', he has chosen them in just the opposite way so that their combination produces the most aggravating clashing and grinding imaginable.[30]

For those in the audience who shared Lalo's view of the music and the choreography, the final section before the end of the first act would have whipped up their feelings even more. The 'Dance of the Earth', just over a minute in duration, is probably the most violent and extreme moment in the whole piece. In their programme book synopsis, the audience would have read the description 'Everyone stamps the earth in ecstasy' but this hugely understates the terrifying energy of this climax of the first act. Just before the 'Dance of the Earth', the frenzy of the music and dance is momentarily silenced as the Sage bows to kiss the earth, accompanied by a slow heartbeat rhythm on the drum and a strange, high chord that seems to come from deep underground. The kiss sets off roars, thrashes and rumblings in the music – this is the section Walt Disney used twenty-five years later in *Fantasia* to depict the earthquake that destroyed the dinosaurs – and it seems that the ruthless forces of nature have been unleashed. With hindsight, it's hard not to read into the rapid machine-gun fire of the trumpets and the crashes and explosions in the percussion a vision of the coming man-made hell of the Great War. Each one of Nijinsky's forty-three dancers is thrown by the violence of the music into cycles of individual repeating movement, lost in what seems like a very modern kind of hell. If Astruc had, indeed, felt the need to go on stage and attempt to restore calm at this point, it is hardly surprising.

The music for the 'Introduction' to the second act, played with the curtain down, set up a peaceful, nocturnal atmosphere. Then, on a rising figure from a solo cello, the curtain went up to reveal the girls acting out a slow, mysterious circle game as a prelude to selecting who among them should be chosen for sacrifice to the sun god Yarilo. But any calm that might have been restored was immediately broken when the audience saw the dancers' pose. The women, clustered together in an outward-facing circle, shuffling round in the now familiar knock-kneed position, had their heads bent to one side, each holding one hand held against their cheek.

This is the point at which the most widely reported heckle of the evening was heard from the audience. 'Get a doctor!' shouted one wit. 'A dentist – they've all got toothache!' shouted another. 'Two dentists!' added a third.[31] These interventions seemed to unleash a new wave of derision as the ballet built inexorably from the 'Glorification of the Chosen One' through the arrival of Ancestors dressed in bearskins towards the sacrificial climax.

But some audience members were, throughout the furore, simply carried away by the power of the work. Carl Van Vechten, an American writer, photographer and friend of Gertrude Stein, described an incident that took place in his box:

> A young man occupied the place behind me. He stood up during the course of the ballet to enable himself to see more clearly. The intense excitement under which he was labouring, thanks to the potent force of the music, betrayed itself presently when he began to beat rhythmically on the top of my head with his fists. My emotion was so great that I did not feel the blows for some time. They were perfectly synchronized with the beat of the music. When I did, I turned around. His apology was sincere. We both had been carried beyond ourselves.[32]

There are conflicting accounts of how the public reacted to the climactic 'Sacrificial Dance', danced by Maria Piltz, who had replaced the pregnant Bronislawa Nijinska. Marie Rambert, dancer and assistant to Nijinsky, remembers that full pandemonium broke out at this point, and Carl Van Vechten recalls Piltz 'executing her strange dance of religious hysteria on a stage dimmed by the blazing light in the auditorium, seemingly to the accompaniment of the disjointed ravings of a mob of angry men and women'. But other reports state that this was the moment when the audience finally calmed down. Romola Pulszky remembered, 'The only moment of relaxation came when the dance of the Chosen Maiden began. It was of such indescribable force, had such beauty, that in its conviction of sacrifice it disarmed even the chaotic audience. They forgot to fight.'[33] Critics afterwards were less complimentary. The characteristically forthright words of Pierre Lalo were typical:

> The poor dancer who plays the sacrificial virgin stands immobile for a good quarter of an hour [*sic*], fixed in the most hideous pose you could imagine: her toes pointed inward, knock-kneed, her body twisted, her neck bent, her head askew; and she only abandons this position to execute a series of clumsy and frantic leaps which make her resemble a disjointed puppet.

As Lalo observed in his review, the 'Sacrificial Dance' was a distillation of the types of stylized movement that had been seen throughout the ballet: knock-kneed trembling, the 'toothache' pose, sawing motions of the arms and a total of 123 jumps. Each cell of movement was repeated in fragments of varying lengths, just like the shards of music for the 'Sacrificial Dance', which Stravinsky seemed to have cut up from a more conventional dance and reassembled, Cubist-style, into something refracted and unpredictable. This was not a realistic, thrashing, dance to the death. It was crueller than that: chilly, robotic, inexorable. It was a pagan ritual for the machine age.

Predictably, at the end of the ballet the house erupted with cheers and catcalls in equal measure, but there are no stories of further disturbances. The artists took five curtain calls and there were special ovations for the orchestra and conductor. Monteux would later say that they had 'played it to the end absolutely as we had rehearsed it in the peace of an empty theatre.'[34] The dancers were exhausted, relieved and, above all, hot. Lydia Sokolova wrote:

I do not know whether it was our wigs, or the smell of our hot flannel costumes. . . or the fact that there were so many of us packed together, or excitement or fear, but we generated heat like a furnace; and at the end of the ballet there can have been none of the forty-odd dancers who was not soaking.[35]

Marie Rambert recalls that the dancers were all far too excited to think of going home. They stayed up all night eating, drinking and running around on the grass and through the trees of the Bois du Boulogne.[36] Jean Cocteau, who also made his way to the Bois after a post-show supper, provided a memorable vignette of the drink-fuelled sentimentality of composer, impresario and choreographer:

At two o'clock in the morning, Stravinsky, Nijinsky, Diaghilev and myself piled into a cab and were driven to the Bois de Boulogne. We kept silent; the night was cool and clear. The odour of the acacias told us we had reached the first trees. Coming to the lakes, Diaghilev, bundled up in opossum, began mumbling in Russian. I could feel Stravinsky and Nijinsky listening attentively and as the coachman lighted his lantern, I saw tears on the impresario's face... you can't imagine the gentleness and the nostalgia of these men, and no matter what Diaghilev may have done after, I shall never forget, in that cab, his great tear-stained face as he recited Pushkin in the Bois de Boulogne.[37]

Stravinsky, speaking many years later, says that the truth was more prosaic:

After the performance we were excited, angry, disgusted and. . . happy. I went with Diaghilev and Nijinsky to a restaurant. So, far from weeping and reciting Pushkin in the Bois de Boulogne as the legend is, Diaghilev's only comment was: 'Exactly what I wanted!' He certainly looked contented. No one could have been quicker to understand the publicity value and he immediately understood the good thing that had happened in that respect. Quite probably he had already thought about the possibility of such a scandal when I first played him the score, months before, in the east-corner ground room of the Grand Hotel in Venice.[38]

Of the many press reviews over the following few days, a few were unreservedly enthusiastic. Florent Schmitt declared Stravinsky 'the new Messiah for whom we have been waiting since Wagner,'[39] while Octave Maus hailed the work as 'a milestone in the history of the theatre'.[40] A significant number of critics, as we have seen, were openly hostile, with particular vitriol being directed towards Nijinsky who, they felt, should stick to being the greatest dancer in the world and stay away from choreography. However, many hedged their bets, acknowledging that they might well end up on the wrong side of history if they were to pass immediate judgement on something so huge, so complex and so new. 'It is very possible that we have here, in fact, a new music,' wrote Georges Pioch. 'But one is tempted to fear for M. Stravinsky and his followers that they have entered a musical Canaan of which they have given us only a glimpse. Let us respect them, therefore, for their independence and daring.'[41]

The reviews that seemed to sting Stravinsky and his collaborators the most were those that implied they were not sincere, that they had set out solely to make fun of a gullible audience. 'The audience is being mocked, and it revolts!' thundered Adolphe Boschot in the conservative *L'Écho de Paris*. In an interview in the literary periodical *Gil Blas* a few days after the premiere, Stravinsky defended the sincerity of the project:

I have done something new, I expected to disconcert a little those who applauded *Petrushka* and *The Firebird*, and I expected the same sympathy. I acted in all conscience and I do not think I was mistaken; the works I have already had performed and which have been well received should be tokens of my sincerity and should show that I had no wish to make an uncomprehending public laugh.[42]

As the year progressed, *The Rite of Spring* continued to be the talk of Paris. Having had time to reflect, the commentators came to a fuller understanding of the true nature – and importance – of the events of 29 May. Writing in August 1913, Jacques Rivière acknowledged that he, for one, had been suffering from Ballets Russes fatigue before the latest season, fearing that the company had started to trade on past glories:

> But all of a sudden one night, there appeared this thing without profit, this refusal to live off the past, this terrifying blow to the very expectations they had themselves implanted in us, this work which changes everything, which changes the very source of our aesthetic judgements and one which we must immediately number among the greats: *The Rite of Spring*.[43]

Meanwhile, the Ballets Russes had moved on. Immediately after the Paris run of five performances, the last of which took place on 13 June, *The Rite of Spring* was performed four times in London. Like their Parisian counterparts, the London critics reacted with a mix of enthusiasm, bafflement and hostility. But there were no riots in the Theatre Royal, Drury Lane. London responded to the shock of *The Rite of Spring* in an altogether more British way. Just up the road from Drury Lane, at the Hippodrome music-hall near Leicester Square, the comedy double act of Billy Merson and James Watts performed a skit in which they played the Russian Ballet dancers Miss Oridkoff Mersonova and Madame Havafollova, said to have been engaged at considerable expense by arrangement with the Governor of Alexandrovsky Prison upon their release from that penitential institution. In their parody, dubbed the 'Danse du Printemps', they attempted to demonstrate, apparently to much hilarity, the difference between ragtime and springtime.

In August 1913, the Ballets Russes company sailed for South America, Diaghilev staying behind in Europe to attend to other business. In Buenos Aires, Nijinsky and Romola Pulszky were secretly married. On hearing the news Diaghilev summarily sacked Nijinsky, his company's greatest star. Although there was a later reconciliation of sorts, Nijinsky never created another ballet for the company, and danced in public for the final time in 1917, shortly after which he fell victim to the mental illness that would afflict him until his death in 1950.

Nijinsky's choreography for *The Rite of Spring* was lost and the London performances in 1913 were the last time it was seen. Millicent Hodson and Kenneth Archer would reconstruct it in the 1980s using a combination of notes made at the time by Stravinsky and Marie Rambert, the accounts of contemporary critics and commentators, the rehearsal drawings of Valentine Gross and three surviving backstage photographs of the dancers.

In November 1913, Astruc went bankrupt. Six months of bold programming had attracted full houses and huge box-office takings, but he had incurred ruinous costs, not least among them Diaghilev's inflated fees. Having hosted, in its short life, the most famous artistic moment of the still-young century, the ideal theatre for a new kind of art was forced to close its doors. In December, Jacques-Émile Blanche, writing a cultural round-up of the year 1913, bitterly lamented the death of the great artistic experiment at the Théâtre des Champs-Élysées: 'In the meantime, let us toss the trapezists to the Maurice Denis ceiling. All we really want are Music Halls.'[44]

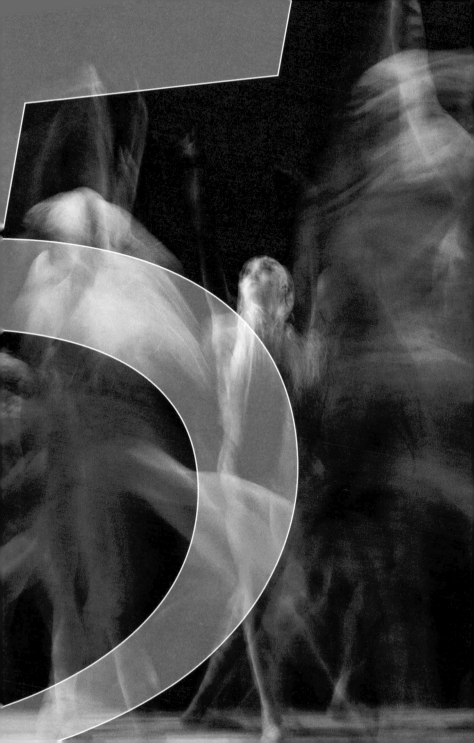

The Music of
The Rite of Spring:
What Was So New?

Who wrote this fiendish *Rite of Spring*?
What right had he to write the thing?
Against our helpless ears to fling
Its crash, clash, cling, clang, bing, bang, bing?

And then to call it *Rite of Spring*?
The season when on joyous wing
The birds melodious carols sing
And harmony's in every thing!

He who could write *The Rite of Spring*
If I be right by right should swing!

Anonymous letter to the *Boston Herald*, 1924[1]

Stravinsky's dream of an ancient ritual to celebrate the coming of spring connected him not just to prehistoric Russia, but to a much more recent tradition. Vivaldi, Beethoven, Schubert, Wagner and many other composers found a seemingly unending source of material in the idea of spring. When Stravinsky was writing *The Rite*, the living rooms of Europe and America were resounding with Norwegian composer Christian Sinding's *Rustle of Spring*, a salon piece popular with amateur pianists because of its relatively undemanding but aurally impressive pyrotechnics. The same year as *The Rite of Spring* premiere in Paris, Leipzig saw the first performance of *On Hearing the First Cuckoo in Spring*, a gorgeous, hazy pastoral on the theme by the English-German composer Frederick Delius. But Stravinsky's spring was a world away from all of this. He was, he said, thinking of 'the violent Russian spring that seemed to begin in an hour and was like the whole Earth cracking. That was the most wonderful event of every year in my childhood.'[2] Stravinsky evoked that violent, brutal version of spring in the astonishing novelty of the musical choices he made for *The Rite*.

There is an intimidating mountain of musicology and analysis written about this half-hour of music: arguably more than about any other musical work. Stravinsky himself deflected discussion about how *The Rite of Spring* actually works: 'I was guided by no system whatsoever in *Le Sacre du printemps* ... I am the vessel through which *Le Sacre* passed.'[3]

This comment by Stravinsky has been much derided. But for the listener, however well informed, there is always a mystery about this music. It will forever be, to some extent, unknowable, and, partly, we want it that way; we want to believe that Stravinsky was simply the vessel for this fully formed miracle that came from somewhere else. But it is, at the same time, irresistible to try to find out as much as possible about how, precisely, the music creates its impact. What was the fuss actually about? Where, specifically, did the innovation lie? Everybody who heard and saw *The Rite of Spring* in 1913, whether they were the musicians playing it, the dancers dancing it or those who were in the audience at the Théâtre des Champs-Élysées, were struck by the same things: chiefly, the unprecedented harmonic dissonances and the complexity of the rhythm. But there were other innovations too: in the structure, the musical architecture of the work; in the way it used melody, and in the orchestration, the actual sound that it made: its crash, clash, cling, clang, bing, bang, bing.

THE ARCHITECTURE OF SPRING

Looking at the score or the track listings on a recording, we see that the work consists of two parts, each with its own 'Introduction'. Part 1 has seven subsequent scenes; Part 2 has five. This is the ballet scenario that Stravinsky and Roerich devised at Talashkino and that provided the basic framework for the music.

The opening bars of the autograph orchestral score
of *The Rite of Spring*.

Le Sacre du Printemps.
Premiere partie
L'adoration de la terre
Igor Strawinsky
poco accelerando
Solo (un peu en dehors)

Part 1: The Adoration of the Earth
Introduction
The Augurs of Spring, Dances of the Young Girls
Ritual of Abduction
Spring Rounds
Ritual of the Rival Tribes
Procession of the Sage
The Sage
Dance of the Earth

Part 2: The Sacrifice
Introduction
Mystic Circles of the Young Girls
Glorification of the Chosen One
Evocation of the Ancestors
Ritual Action of the Ancestors
Sacrificial Dance (The Chosen One)

As we've seen, Stravinsky quickly distanced himself from the dramatic scenario and, soon after the premiere, began to refer to *The Rite* as a symphonic work for the concert hall. But what kind of symphony is this? *The Rite of Spring* could not be further from the rational, symphonic arguments of Haydn, Beethoven, Brahms and the Austro-German tradition. Although there seems to be an enormous amount of movement in the piece, it does not seem to go anywhere, it does not move from A to B, grow from one state to the other, from struggle to triumph, from darkness to light, in the way that a symphony by Beethoven or Tchaikovsky or Mahler would. It simply exists. *The Rite of Spring*'s musical materials are assembled in blocks that are cut and spliced together to create a fragmented reality, as in film or as with the Cubism of Stravinsky's contemporaries Picasso and Braque. Some have likened this handling of material to mosaic technique. The composer George Benjamin has described Stravinsky's approach to his material in *The Rite* as 'the juxtaposition of bald, primitivistic panels'.[4] Esa-

Pekka Salonen used the analogy of a game of dominos where pieces can be joined together or repeated according to an arcane set of rules that we need never know.[5] This 'block' principle is immediately apparent even to those who cannot read music. To open the pages of Stravinsky's manuscript score is to look at the carefully drawn pages of a designer, with architectural blocks of different sizes and densities placed next to or on top of each other, some of them expanded or contracted versions of the same thing, others in total contrast or in counterpoint – but the boundaries between the different musical objects are always clear-cut; there are no soft edges. The different scenes of the ballet are self-contained, with very little development of motifs between sections, although a chunk of music might insert itself in the middle of a scene as a sudden cinematic flashback or flash-forward to another scene. In ballet music up to that point, there were transitions, fluid music of transformation as one scene dissolved into another. In *The Rite* there is no connective tissue: the transitions are sudden, brutal and absolute.

MELODY, OLD AND NEW

Some who heard the premiere in May 1913 complained that *The Rite of Spring* had no tunes, no melody to hang on to. This perception is probably due to the sheer volume of aural information coming at the listener on first hearing. In fact *The Rite of Spring* is full of tunes. Some are slow and plaintive, like the opening solo bassoon melody or the 'Mystic Circles of the Young Girls' tune near the start of Part 2; others are fast, jagged and aggressive, like 'Ritual of Abduction' or 'Ritual of the Rival Tribes' in Part 1. All are singable; most are simple, and almost all have more than a whiff of folk music about them. Possibly because he was keen to preserve the idea that *The Rite* came to him out of nowhere, in a dream, Stravinsky was coy about admitting any borrowings from folk music: the opening bassoon solo melody is, he said, the only folk tune in the work – a wedding song he had found in a collection of Lithuanian folk melodies.

In the 1970s, Stravinsky's friend the writer Lawrence Morton took the trouble to seek out the Lithuanian collection, which had been published by the Polish monk Anton Juszkiewicz in Kraków in 1900. He found that Stravinsky had used more of these tunes than he admitted, some almost unaltered, some fragmented, most transformed rhythmically, but all recognizable. Other melodies in *The Rite*, with their simple four- or five-note shapes, sound like folk music but cannot be traced to the Juszkiewicz anthology. We can only speculate if Stravinsky found them elsewhere – perhaps from Sergey Kolosov, the *gusli*-player who played to him and Roerich at Talashkino – or if he composed them himself. Perhaps it doesn't matter where the melodies came from: it could be argued that folk tunes are just raw material like anything else in *The Rite of Spring*, to be manipulated and transformed to make something startling and new. But there is no doubt that the use of folk melodies, either genuinely ancient or newly composed, is one of the aspects of *The Rite* that roots it deep in the past and connects it to shared human experience. And, as we shall see, the 'otherness' of these folk tunes in relation to Western classical music makes possible many of Stravinsky's innovations.

HARMONY AND DISSONANCE

Leonard Bernstein said that *The Rite of Spring* contained the best dissonances that anyone ever wrote.[6] Dissonance in music means the simultaneous sounding of two or more notes that would not, under the conventions of classical harmony, go together. In the European classical tradition, from Purcell to Bach, Haydn to

Beethoven, Brahms to Mahler, dissonance was liberally used, but to very specific expressive effect. It was a passing state on the way to consonance, a tension to be resolved, a knot to be untangled, a dark cloud that would, always, dissolve to reveal light.

The major and minor – diatonic – scales, which form the scaffolding of classical harmony, contain these hierarchies and tensions within them. The terms that we use for the notes of the diatonic scale are all about the pecking order: tonic (the keynote), dominant, subdominant, mediant, leading note. The grammar of classical harmony depends on the gravitational pull of one note or chord on another, according to their place in this pecking order. Satisfactory resolution is finally achieved only when the most important note, the tonic, is reached.

As early as the 1860s, Wagner had played with the harmonic expectations of listeners with the ambiguous gravitational pull in the famous 'Tristan chord'.* By the turn of the twentieth century, when Mahler was writing his later symphonies, harmonic gratification had become ever more deferred – as in the *Adagietto* of his Fifth Symphony, with its aching, long-breathed phrases that seem to linger on a dissonance for ever before finally, inevitably, coming to resolution. Whatever happens along the way, we still know where the music is going; we are certain that resolution will eventually come.

In Berlin at the time, Arnold Schoenberg was speaking of 'the emancipation of the dissonance'. Schoenberg declared that all notes were now equal, and, since there was no longer a hierarchy, no resolution was necessary. Stravinsky travelled to Berlin just as he was completing *The Rite*, met Schoenberg and heard his *Pierrot lunaire*. Pierrot is a suite of twenty-one compressed, cabaret

---

* The chord at the beginning of *Tristan und Isolde* that, with its pile-up of so-called augmented intervals, is highly ambiguous and disorienting to listeners accustomed to classical harmonic language.

miniatures: a singer-actor intones the intense, Expressionistic songs of a moonstruck clown while a chamber ensemble plays terse, crystalline music in which all twelve notes of the scale float and shimmer, free of any harmonic gravitational pull or any hint of major or minor harmonies. Stravinsky was impressed, but he was not tempted down that path – at least not yet.*

Yet early listeners to *The Rite of Spring* were struck by the dissonant harmonies. After the first performance, the critic Pierre Lalo wrote:

> This is the most dissonant music ever written. . . I say to you. . . that the system and cult of the wrong note have never been practised with so much zeal and so continuously as in this score; that from the first bar to the last, whatever note one expects, it is never that note that comes, but the next-door note, the note that ought not to come; whatever chord may seem to be implied by the preceding chord, it is a different chord that happens. . . these are not pretty harmonies, elegant chords, combined with patient subtlety. They are hard, strong, abundant harmonies, invented freely by a harsh and fecund musical nature. This music has nothing in common with what our most recent composers have been writing.[7]

Lalo's vivid words have often been quoted to illustrate the outrage that *The Rite* evoked at its premiere. But a careful reading of what he actually wrote shows that he was full of admiration for the radically new but somehow coherent harmonic world that Stravinsky had created. Stravinsky had side-stepped the goal-oriented, gravitational approach of the Austro-German music tradition and found something different. He did not follow

---

* It was only after Schoenberg's death in 1951 that Stravinsky began to incorporate some of the Viennese composer's ideas into his music and used elements of the twelve-tone or 'serial' method of composition, which Schoenberg had developed in the 1920s.

Schoenberg and opt for total dissonance at all times, avoiding consonant harmonies. Lalo's review talks about chords implying other chords: *The Rite of Spring* is full of familiar chords, but they do not do what you expect them to.

The boldest, simplest way Stravinsky used to create dissonance was to take a conventional chord and play it at the same time as another conventional chord in a key bearing a dissonant relationship to the first chord: the clearest example is the bitonal E flat7/E chord that pounds through most of the 'Augurs of Spring' section near the beginning of the ballet – two consonant chords a dissonant semitone apart. Played separately, the chords sound consonant; played together they create crunching dissonance, but one in which the listener can still perceive the two familiar objects glinting through the noise.

Musicologists have suggested that an important source for Stravinsky's new harmonic world was through the use, whether consciously or not, of the unusual harmonic properties of the octatonic scale. He would have learned the secrets of this scale from his teacher Nikolai Rimsky-Korsakov who often associated its strange qualities with magic, sorcery and mystery. Mussorgsky used it in *Boris Godunov*, and Stravinsky in his first two Russian ballets, *The Firebird* and *Petrushka*. It became known as the 'Russian scale', but it was not limited to Russians. In 1879, the French aristocrat and amateur composer Prince Edmond de Polignac published a treatise on the possibilities of octatonic harmony and Debussy was seduced by its possibilities, using octatonic scales and whole-tone scales (see below) mixed with diatonic harmony to create the uprooted, floating quality in his music. In the twentieth century, Olivier Messiaen referred to it as 'the second mode of limited transposition' and used it as an important colour in his music.[8] Jazz musicians such as Charlie Parker and Thelonious Monk called it the diminished scale and used it liberally to generate a strikingly modern sound in melody and harmony. Hollywood composers reached for the octatonic scale to conjure up other-worldliness or dark forces. The rock bands King Crimson and Radiohead have based songs on its unsettling intervals.

The reason for this uprooted, floating, unsettled quality is that, unlike major and minor scales, the octatonic scale is a symmetrical structure – it divides the octave into eight steps, strictly alternating whole steps and half steps – tone, semitone, tone, semitone, etc. (Major and minor scales have a non-symmetrical distribution of tones and semitones, creating their inherent hierarchies and tensions.) The 'great dissonances' in *The Rite* that Bernstein referred to can be easily found inside the octatonic scale and, at the same time, many familiar harmonies are found there too: major, minor and diminished chords. But, unlike in the diatonic scale, these chords do not feel closely related to each other in classical terms; there is no hierarchy or gravitational pull between them or towards a keynote. So, to the ear accustomed to Western classical harmony, the octatonic scale gives us familiar chords but in unfamiliar relationships with each other.

Octatonic harmony appears throughout *The Rite*, but Stravinsky combines it with many other harmonic elements to create his alternative sound world. The folk melodies themselves, with their ancient modes, push Stravinsky into thinking outside classical harmonic convention. And throughout *The Rite*, another alternative scale, the whole-tone scale, makes occasional appearances. As its name suggests, this scale is another symmetrical structure; it appears in the music of Debussy and Bartok. (Stevie Wonder uses it in the ascending scale in the introduction to 'You are the Sunshine of My Life'.) The most striking use of the whole-tone scale appears in the 'Dance of the Earth', which closes the first part of the ballet and where an ascending whole-tone scale gradually emerges from the bottom of the orchestra, getting louder and louder as it repeats before it appears to swallow the music whole.

Throughout the work, even in its most dissonant passages, the listener perceives familiar musical objects. And therein lies the key to why *The Rite of Spring*, after the initial shock and despite all the dissonance, became a popular work in the concert hall, while Schoenberg's music from the same period remains more elusive for audiences. With Stravinsky, the familiar tonal objects – chords, melodies, ostinatos* – are still there; they are just arranged in a spectacularly novel way.

FINDING THE RHYTHMS OF THE EARTH

On the morning of the premiere of *The Rite of Spring*, Diaghilev's press release promised the public 'the most startling polyrhythms ever produced by the brain of a musician', and it is the rhythmic innovation that, above all else, carries the violence and terror of the piece. In a letter to Roerich written when Stravinsky was halfway through *The Rite*, it is clear that he felt there was something mystical in the way the rhythms of spring had been revealed to him as he was composing: 'Throughout the whole composition I give the listener a sense of the closeness of the people to the earth, of the commonality of their lives with the earth, by means of lapidary rhythms.'[9]

From a rhythmic point of view, *The Rite of Spring* starts deceptively: the 'Introduction' is the only moment in the entire piece that is rhythmically free, not driven by a pulse. The melodic lines in the 'Introduction' interweave as if they are being improvised, drawn freehand in the air. But for the rest of the work,

---

* A short pattern of music that repeats.

pulse, rhythm and metre dominate every section of the music, and Stravinsky constantly confounds the listener's rhythmic expectations. In the same way that classical music had set up expectations in harmony, there were also rhythmic patterns and structures in which listeners felt comfortable, originating mostly from the repetitive human movements of walking, dancing or working. Repeating groupings of two, three or four in the bar, with a tendency to accent the first beat in each group, was standard and, on a larger level, those bars were usually grouped into phrases in multiples of four. From a Beethoven symphony to a twenty-first-century pop song, this is the norm.

But when Stravinsky was looking for the deep rhythms of the earth, he uncovered patterns that were more fearsome and less predictable. The starkest example of this comes in the first dance of the ballet, 'The Augurs of Spring', a brutal shock after the rhythmic looseness of the 'Introduction'. A heavy, stamping beat in a regular metre of two in the bar pounds through the entire scene. But this regular beat is slashed into by ferocious accents that come at entirely unpredictable places.

Another way in which *The Rite* upsets the rhythmic apple cart is via the simple adding or subtracting of beats from a pattern as it repeats. This device has both ancient and modern roots. On one hand, there is a clear connection with folk melodies, which often freely expand or contract by a beat or two to fit in words. But this is also a Cubist approach to rhythm, a refracted reality, a very twentieth-century interrupted narrative. In the final 'Sacrificial Dance', where the Chosen One dances herself to death, it is as if Stravinsky has composed a repetitive, whirling dance for her and then cut it up into fragments, each of which is of a slightly different length and is repeated at unexpected intervals. The reassembled dance is fractured, halting, unsure of itself – and devastating.

In other places, Stravinsky creates rhythmic complexity by taking relatively simple musical patterns of differing lengths and speeds and layering them on top of each other. (This has much in common with traditional African music but, while we know that Picasso was looking at African sculpture at this time, there is no evidence that Stravinsky had encountered African rhythms.) In the middle of the 'Ritual of the Rival Tribes', leading into the 'Procession of the Sage', the music builds up to a huge cacophony as repeating phrases of different lengths are laid over each other. The effect is like some giant, deafening machine with cogs and pistons of varying sizes operating at varying speeds and rates of repetition. These may be the deep rhythms of nature, but they are also those of the industrial twentieth century.

SONIC POWER

The acoustic range of *The Rite of Spring* is enormous, from the single, high bassoon melody that emerges out of silence at the very beginning of the work to the fearsome noise of the 'Procession of the Sage' or the clamour of the 'Dance of the Earth' that follows it. A key decision any composer makes in starting a new piece is in designing the sound that it will make, and which instruments to use. In this respect, Stravinsky was not particularly revolutionary. *The Rite* is written for what is, essentially, a late-Romantic symphony orchestra with strings, wind, brass and percussion. The orchestra is large – the biggest Stravinsky had used to date or, indeed, would ever use – but not exceptionally so given the maximalist standards of the times: Mahler's Eighth, the so-called 'Symphony of a Thousand', had been performed in 1910 with gargantuan orchestral and vocal forces, and Schoenberg's *Gurrelieder* had been premiered in Vienna earlier in 1913 with a similarly enormous line-up. But Stravinsky was able to create maximum acoustic impact because of some specific instrumental choices he made and his revolutionary use of the instruments of the orchestra.

In the hierarchy of a Romantic orchestra, the strings are the most important, carrying the melodies and the emotional core of the music. In *The Rite of Spring* orchestra, this is not the case. The strings are subordinated to winds, brass and percussion. Stravinsky does, from time to time, give them tunes, but the strings seldom appear, as they do in nineteenth-century music, as a whole, resonant group. They are often divided up to perform a variety of functions: they are used as accompaniment, adding colour or depth to music that is happening elsewhere, or they have a rhythmic and percussive role. At the opening of 'The Augurs of Spring', the lower strings thump out the repetitive 'Augurs' chord with heavy downbows and thick, bitonal harmony. The ear could be tricked into thinking it was hearing a giant drum.

The woodwind and brass sections were large, with instruments added in the extreme high and low registers. So, at the top end, Stravinsky added small, high clarinets in D and E flat, two piccolos to the flute section, and a high D trumpet to the brass; at the bottom end, there were alto flute, two bass clarinets, contrabassoon, bass trumpet and two bass tubas. Thus *The Rite* matched its extremes of quiet and loud with extremes of high and low. And, just as the strings played against type, the winds did unexpected things also: the opening, high bassoon melody puzzled the first-night audiences because it was playing way out of its normal range – what *was* this unearthly sound? – and the trumpets, historically reserved for loud fanfares, are given one of the quietest moments in the entire work – a bleak little duet in the 'Introduction' to Part 2.

There are some surprising omissions from *The Rite* orchestra: harp, piano and celesta were part of the luxuriant orchestral sound of the ballet of the time, and Stravinsky had used them to add lustre in *The Firebird* and *Petrushka*. But perhaps these were too decorative, too gilded for this pagan ritual. The percussion section of the orchestra was a more suitable arsenal to employ for the brutal sound of the Russian spring. But it is surprising that Stravinsky's percussion section is relatively small: orchestras normally use only four players for *The Rite*; Edgard Varèse's orchestral composition *Amériques*, written just five years later, demanded eleven percussionists. In Stravinsky's percussion section, the tam-tam, the guiro (a Latin American scraping instrument) and the bass drum combine to create the cataclysmic noise-music of the 'Procession of the Sage' and the 'Dance of the Earth'. But it is the two sets of timpani that propel the energy of the piece at key moments, most significantly in the final 'Sacrificial Dance' where their unrelenting blows repeatedly keep on unleashing the the cyclic cruelty of the sacrifice of a young girl.

If the percussion section plays a big role in generating the violence of *The Rite of Spring*, the most innovative and striking way that Stravinsky achieves the unprecedented sonic power of the piece is in the places where he repurposes the entire orchestra into a kind of huge, virtual percussion instrument. There are many examples of this. We have already looked at the way in which the strings sound like a gigantic drum in the 'Augurs of Spring' section. The fierce jabs that randomly cut across that beat are not created by percussion but by all eight horns playing *staccato* chords, sounding for all the world like thwacks on a louder, drier drum. Likewise, in the closing 'Sacrificial Dance' where the orchestra repeatedly plays clusters of thick, dissonant chords mostly in rhythmic unison, each spasm is set off by a blow on the timpani. As the horror of the final sacrifice plays itself out, the whole orchestra has become percussion-like: pitch is subordinated to rhythm; music is becoming noise.

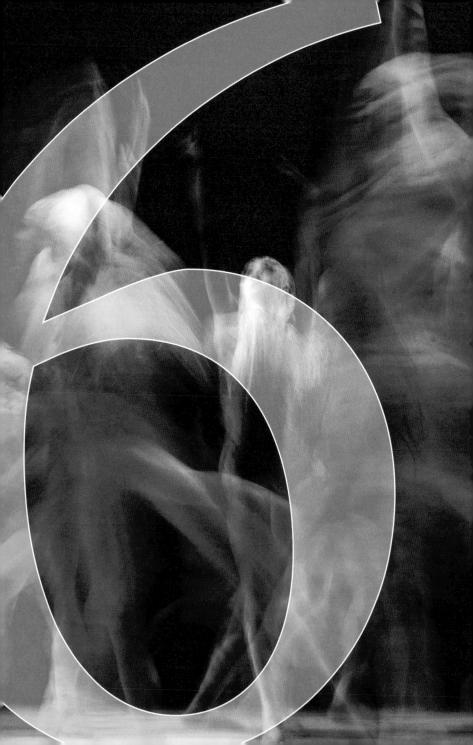

The Rite
Step by Step:
A Listening Guide

This scene-by-scene listening guide to *The Rite of Spring* is best read in conjunction with listening to a recording. Most recordings are arranged with separate tracks relating to the scenes of the ballet. The scenes are short, ranging between around forty seconds and around four-and-a-half minutes long, making it straightforward to follow the music from the description. For the purposes of orientation in the scenario, and for historical colour, some references have been made to the reconstruction of Nijinsky's original choreography by Millicent Hodson and Kenneth Archer.

PART 1: THE ADORATION OF THE EARTH

Introduction

The Rite of Spring opens with a long, lonely, high note on a bassoon out of which, eventually, a single line of melody falls and then rises again, like a Stone Age piper improvising from a distant hill. The tune is soon coloured by a rocking motive on the horn and a pair of clarinets slithering in parallel down a scale. A fanfare call on a cor anglais answers the bassoon, growing in confidence and stretching itself out into a melody as other wind instruments cluster around it, and the music starts to sound like the swarm of Russian reed pipes (*dudki*) that Stravinsky described. Stravinsky said at another time that this 'Introduction' was like the awakening of nature,[2] and nature indeed appears to stir when a loud, plucked flourish in the strings shoots a bolt of energy upwards through the orchestra, setting off the sounds of birdcalls, insects buzzing, flutterings of wings. The music, still played predominantly by the wind instruments, grows and swells and deflates like bellows, gains rhythm and pulse with the throbbing of lower strings and bass clarinets. Order makes an attempt to establish itself out of the chaos with assertive call and response between single instruments and choruses of winds. This builds to a climax and abruptly cuts off. The solo bassoon is back with the same melody, this time settled a tone lower. A clarinet trill introduces a shard of ticking ostinato plucked loudly on violins – a foreign, mechanical object in this organic nature world. A downward improvisatory flourish on clarinets is a last shudder of the chaos. A ghostly chord on six violas is handed seamlessly to another on horns and clarinets and the shard of ostinato is back. At this point on the manuscript score, the word *rideau* (curtain up) is written by hand in blue pencil.

The Augurs of Spring – Dances of the Young Girls

The strings pound out the heavy beats of the dissonant 'Augurs' chord with the horns dealing the unpredictable blows. After a few bars of pounding, the music cuts to the ticking ostinato from the 'Introduction', this time on cor anglais. We realize that this ostinato, together with the plucked cello in the bass line, is a skeleton version of the 'Augurs' chord – with the fast bassoon figures in the middle adding another, octatonic harmonic colour – and that it will propel this dance to the end. The pounding chords return. In Nijinsky's choreography, the tribes of men on the stage have been forced into a repetitive machine dance by this rhythm. The old Sorceress, who has been stock-still the while, is now jolted into life by high slashes in the winds and runs around the stage looking for signs of spring with her birch twigs. The critic Émile Vuillermoz described the effect of the music on Nijinsky's dancers: 'It throws them in the air, burns their soles. The interpreters of Stravinsky are not simply electrified by these rhythmic discharges; they are electrocuted.'[3]

overleaf
The Forefathers by Nicholas Roerich, 1912: a characteristic portrayal of an imagined prehistory, in which people lived in harmony with nature.

Then follows a build-up of folk melodies: the bassoons introduce a spiky, grandfatherly tune that is played over the ticking ostinato and imitated mockingly by the other wind instruments. It is dramatically interrupted by a crash on timpani and low brass, only for the ticking ostinato to recover by slicing through the music from top to bottom in a giant, cut-up version of itself. Re-established, it is then joined by a new folk-like tune, twisting and sinuous on solo horn. At this point in Nijinsky's ballet, the young girls come up from the river to join their dance, a stately *khorovod* played here like a hymn in parallel thirds on the brass, soon joined by triangle and antique cymbals to give it warmth and sparkle. The injection of feminine energy makes the tension in the music rise and the climax of the dance, with the whole orchestra in a whirling, pulsing dance, with tunes and ostinatos layered and multiplied, a big new whole-tone-scale bass line in the brass and priapic horn whoops bringing the dance to a pitch of what can only be erotic frenzy.

Ritual of Abduction

In the story of the ballet, the young people play a game in which the men try to kidnap the women, a ritualized rehearsal for what will happen for real at the end. But the music here tells us that this game of chase is, in fact, pitiless and terrifying. The action is set off by violent crashes on the bass drum and timpani triggering a jagged, running theme in the winds that chases itself through the orchestra. Lawrence Morton has identified this theme as one of the Lithuanian folk tunes,[4] but there is no lingering to enjoy it. This is frenetic, menacing music of pursuit: hunting horns sound the alarm and the constantly shifting metres add to the atmosphere of fear. Special instrumental effects that, with twenty-first-century hindsight, we associate with cinematic tension, are liberally used: *tremolando* strings, rapid double-tonguing on the trumpets and flutes – and the sense of unease is heightened by the uprooted octatonic harmony. We hear a flash-forward to the 'Ritual of the Rival Tribes' as the orchestra comes together in rhythmic unison at the climax, but this does little to dispel the terror and, towards the end of the scene, the strings seem to be cornered, going round in circles with the chase theme, while the orchestra deals great hammer-blows. But out of this violence emerges a long, high trill on the violins that provides a way out.

Spring Rounds

The flute takes over the high trills and the texture clears. Against the trills, a spacious, slow incantation is played in open octaves on clarinets. Lawrence Morton tells us that this incantation is made up from two of the Lithuanian folk tunes, cut and spliced together. 'Spring Rounds' is the scene where *The Rite of Spring* is most explicit in its Russian folklore roots. It is a *khorovod*, a singing, walking, dancing game of lines and circles with a distant pagan history. When the spacious incantation breaks off, the dance begins in earnest. The bottom end of the orchestra starts a heavy, repeating accompaniment riff whose rhythmic undertow seems to be both pushing and dragging the dance simultaneously like a deep, wheezing accordion. Nijinsky had his dancers repeatedly bow to the ground to illustrate the depth in this music, which is interrupted a couple of times by interjections of high piping woodwinds in *dudki* mode. Then the three repeated top notes of the accompaniment riff become a melody played in parallel thirds like a *khorovod* might be sung; we recognize it as a flashback to the tune foretold in the 'Dances of the Young Girls' two scenes earlier. Like so much of *The Rite*, the material is treated in a mosaic, cut-up manner: the *dudki* interjections are blocks of the same music but of differing sizes;

the *khorovod* melody is full of internal repetitions and unexpected lengthenings and shortenings, seeming to get stuck on individual notes and figures. At the climax of the scene, a huge percussion crash sets in motion a more frightening version of the *khorovod* tune , which is now shrieked out by the entire orchestra, soured by snarling dissonances and getting ever more stuck in the groove of its internal patterns. A sudden and brief flashback to the terror music of the 'Ritual of Abduction' cuts, equally abruptly, back to the calm of the high incantation from the beginning of the scene.

Ritual of the Rival Tribes – Procession of the Sage

We are catapulted into a violent wargame between the two tribes. This is perhaps the most straightforwardly illustrative music in the ballet, a cinematic fight scene. It announces itself with a loud, pugilistic gesture on timpani and low brass, then cuts to a block of punchy, *staccato* music on winds and strings that is then answered by a bigger, stronger version of itself from elsewhere in the orchestra. And so the battle continues until a new element, a smooth, folk tune, again thickened out with folky parallel thirds, is introduced and passed around the instruments. The punchy, *staccato* fight music returns, underpinned and emboldened by a brutish, pounding bass, and it takes over the whole orchestra; at this point in the original choreography, Nijinsky's warring tribes are dancing together, in a ferocious unison, perhaps united against a greater force about to appear. When the smooth folk tune returns, it is joined by a strange, foreign element: a long-breathed, repeating melody in a clashing tonality played on the particularly penetrating sound of two tenor and two bass tubas. This heralds the arrival of the Sage, the Oldest and Wisest One. It also sets off the nightmarish musical machine that ends this scene as musical patterns of different lengths and speeds whirr, clang, scrape and spin against each other while the strange tuba tune of the Sage marches on through the middle of the music, relentless and oblivious. Similarly, Nijinsky's dancers have been thrown by the terror of the Sage into their own individualized mechanical movement patterns, each lost in his own repetitive, nightmarish world.

The Sage

This turning point in the ballet lasts for a mere twenty-five seconds or so – four bars of music. A quiet chord is held on bassoons: from another bassoon and two double-basses comes an iambic heartbeat rhythm, played four times. In the ballet, all eyes are on the old Sage who bows down to kiss the earth; as he does so, the earth quietly sings back a ghostly chord.

Dance of the Earth

The old man's earth kiss unleashes mayhem. A low rumble on the bass drum swells, in a split second, into a seismic roar that propels us into the 'Dance of the Earth'. The thunderous drumming never lets up until the end of the scene, driving along just over a minute of perpetual motion. Across the top of one of the sketch pages for this section, Stravinsky wrote, 'There is music wherever there is rhythm, as there is life wherever there is a pulse.' Also on the sketches for this section he has written out two melodies that, although we do not know their source, appear to be folk tunes. Looking at the score, these two tunes are certainly to be found, but the sheer speed and violence of the music means that they are barely identifiable to the ear. They have lost any expressive, folk characteristics they might have had and, at this point, they are used simply as material for generating this terrifying climax to the first half. One of them scurries through the middle of the music like a speeded-up jig, keeping the dance motoring on. The second, an innocent-looking tune with a whole-tone-scale feel, is fractured to become the heavily disguised source of the rapid machine-gun-fire brass and wind music at the start. It must surely have been this section that Jacques-Émile Blanche recalled during the air-raids of the 'Cubist war' not long after. The second folk tune also generates the rising whole-tone-scale bass line that, we notice only gradually, underpins the whole scene. Towards the end of this terrifying minute or so of music, the tubas magnify this ascending bass line, which now appears to be emerging from the core of the earth to devour the music. At that point, we cut to silence.

PART 2: THE SACRIFICE

Introduction

Day has turned to night. The 'Introduction' to Part 2, played in the original ballet with the curtain down, is both bewitching night music and a foreshadowing of the brutality to come. Some of the richest harmonies in the piece are found here. The music starts with gentle rocking between two minor chords a whole tone apart (E flat minor and C sharp minor). But they are enrobed in a hushed, sustained chord of D minor on horns and oboes. D minor is the most dissonant chord possible in relation to the other two but, far from sounding harsh, like the bitonal clash of the 'Augurs' chord, Stravinsky's use of spacing and orchestration gives this dissonance a rich, upholstered quality. It is the thick harmony of night. As these dense harmonies start to move around and surge and fall, the beginnings of a slow folk song float in on high strings, foretelling the plaintive tune that will accompany the mysterious circle games of the young girls in the next scene. The young girls' tune then becomes clothed in the thick harmony of the opening and is passed between sections of the orchestra, only to be interrupted by music that is almost shocking in its quietness: a tightly interwoven sliver of a duet for trumpets. The trumpet duet music is then taken up by other instruments and surrounded by a nocturnal version of the dawn stirrings of nature from the very opening of the piece: a repeating upward call on clarinet like a night bird, and rustlings, scratchings and shudderings all around. After another faint echo of the young girls' tune on the horns, marked *très lointain* in the score, the trumpet-duet music is heard for the last time, now down in the murky depths of the orchestra. Out of this gloom rises a single bar of cello solo of startling sweetness. At this point, the word *rideau* is written on the manuscript, this time in green pencil.

Mystic Circles of the Young Girls

The curtain rises on the young girls standing in a circle 'as if welded together', in Stravinsky's words. This is another circle game, but the stakes are higher: this time, the one who is 'out' must die. The young girl's tune from the Part 2 'Introduction' is the first music we hear, scored strangely for divided violas accompanied by a guitar-like plucking on the cellos. Out of the end of the tune emerges a chord on sour muted horns that will return with a more explicitly malign function later in this scene. A tense clarinet trill and rising *tremolando* strings reinforce the sense of dread, and introduce a new folk-like tune on the alto flute, which, to add to the unease, is then repeated, doubled in highly dissonant major sevenths like an out-of-tune organ. The new tune becomes established before being cut off abruptly. The lower strings lay down a drumbeat. Stravinsky's notes to Nijinsky ask for 'a bell-swinging movement' from the dancers at this point, and the new falling tune that comes in here is a slow tolling, ding-dong figure. It cuts again to the young girls' melody as they hunch together again and slowly turn in their circle. But this time, when the music freezes on the muted horn chord, given an added sting by a sharp pluck on the cellos, one of the girls falls on the floor. The circling starts again; the music freezes on the horn chord again; the girl falls again. She has lost the game; she is the Chosen One. The horns and trumpets sound the alarm, the music hurtles upwards in fast scales about to go out of control, and then it crashes together on eleven devastating hammer-blows.

Glorification of the Chosen One

In Nijinsky's ballet, the Chosen One stands frozen still in the centre of the circle, but the girls who surround her are thrown into repeating patterns of movement by the savage rhythms of the music. The 'Glorification' is the last orgiastic music in the ballet – the final 'Sacrificial Dance' is, for the most part, taut and controlled in comparison, and all the more brutal for being so. Here, the rhythmic daring of *The Rite* is at its most naked: the musicians are counting two bars in 5, the next in 7, the next in 3, the next in 4 and so on. It is also perhaps the most pronounced example of the mosaic or domino style of moving around musical material before we get to the 'Sacrificial Dance'. Five different ideas are repeated and intercut with each other in unpredictable ways. The first block, which opens the dance, is an upward sweep followed by a downward run, the whole thing pushed off the ground by a lopsided bass notes in 5 metre. This gesture throws the dancers into the air in Nijinsky's choreography every time it appears. The second block of material is an *oom-cha* figure on strings, horns and oboes – it's easy to imagine Stravinsky hammering this out on his boarding house piano; the third is a varied, descending version of the *oom-cha*; the fourth is the upward, fast scales from just before the eleven blows in the previous scene; and the fifth is a screaming brassy section with vertiginous glissandi on the strings. All of these slabs of music are cut to different sizes and moved around to make this distorted, disconnected, Cubist dance in honour of the doomed girl.

Evocation of the Ancestors

As so often happens with other sections, the 'Glorification' dance does not end but is brutally cut off in mid-air and we find ourselves thrown into the next scene. A flourish on drums and the low instruments of the orchestra takes us down to a low, sustained D sharp that provides a deep underpinning for the whole of this short movement. Just as Nijinsky's dancers were thrown into the air by the upward scream in the orchestra in the last section, so they are floored by this downward blow. Above the sustained bass note, a choir of wind and brass blazes out a hymn-like chant, harmonized in bright C major-centred chords, confident enough to summon up the ancients. The choirs of instruments take up the chant in different parts of the orchestra, as if from near and far and, as we might expect, the rhythms are irregular, cut up, unpredictable.

Ritual Action of the Ancestors

The Ancestors circle round the Chosen One to prepare the ground for the sacrifice. Strings and horns, once again reimagined as drums, combine with the percussion section to make a soft drumbeat with an offbeat tambourine to which the ancients, clad in bearskins, pad around the stage. The cor anglais slithers upwards in a snake-charmer-like melody, soon joined by the alto flute adding to the heavy air of mystery. A new tune appears, like a distant procession played on the strange, hollow sound of low trumpets and bass trumpet. Richard Taruskin has related this tune, with its simple, four-note, falling shape, to a type of western Russian song for the invocation of spring. In a flashback to what happens with the *khorovod* tune in 'Spring Rounds', the processional tune is suddenly magnified, shrieked out by the whole orchestra, soured by dissonant workings going on in the middle of the texture. It breaks off but is soon back, this time even louder, even more dissonant with high, skirling winds and strings and the full arsenal of percussion. Again, the music is cut off abruptly and we are back to the opening drumbeat and the snake-charmer tune, this time on bass trumpet. When the bass clarinet starts its improvisatory flurries around the drumbeat, at one point stopping it in its tracks, we sense that something big is about to happen. A *staccato* scale rushes downwards on the bass clarinet. Stravinsky's sketch for this scale is followed by 'The End', written in pencil. It's hard to believe, but the composer briefly entertained the idea of placing the 'Sacrificial Dance' before this music and having *The Rite of Spring* tail off, *pianissimo*, at the bottom of a bass-clarinet scale. But he had second thoughts, and the bass-clarinet run became the portal through which we are hurled, headlong, into the final catastrophe.

Sacrificial Dance – The Chosen One

The 'Sacrificial Dance' is all the more frightening because of its relative restraint. Like the 'Glorification of the Chosen One', it is a fractured, Cubist dance but, this time, the constant cuts and pauses appear more deliberate, more cruel and more catastrophic. It is the

A reproduction of Valentine Hugo's sketches from the rehearsal drawings depicting 'The Final Sacrificial Dance of the Chosen One', with fragments of the music from that section, published in *Montjoie!* magazine, June 1913.

longest section in the ballet but the music is, in comparison with other sections, not especially fast, not especially loud and, barring one brief episode, not especially frenzied. For most of the dance there is no counterpoint: the orchestra is in rhythmic unison, its entire percussive power focused, disciplined, closed in tightly on the victim. The dance announces itself with taut, repeated chords played by the string section on *staccato* downbows, much like the percussive 'Augurs' chord in the first scene. This chord is also similar in harmonic structure to the 'Augurs' chord: a D7 mixed with E flat; once again, two consonant chords a semitone apart, making for a percussive dissonance.

The music for this recurring opening section of the 'Sacrificial Dance' is made up of short motives or cells that expand and contract in length as they are repeated and intercut with one another. Watching the reconstruction of Nijinsky's choreography is a good way to see this structure in action. Nijinsky's Chosen One finds four types of movement for each of four cells of music. The first type of movement is for the opening repeated chords, each of which propels her into the air with both legs kicking back from the knees; the second, a three-note descending figure that always follows the repeated chords makes her turn to her right, lifting both arms; the third is a high, brassy, five-note fanfare figure on which her right arm makes a whirring motion as she leaps, and the fourth is another high brass figure, sometimes two sometimes three notes long, which sees her running towards the edge of the circle of Ancestors in a break for freedom. The short phrases are jolted into action by blows from the bottom of the orchestra: double-basses and timpani.

After only thirty seconds or so of this taut, Cubist dance, the texture abruptly changes: the real percussion drops out and the low winds and strings become, once again, a virtual drum, pounding out a low beat. In this section we see Nijinsky's Chosen

One shaking in fear in the centre of the circle to the virtual drumbeats and attempting another escape each time the sharp, stabbing, descending figures on winds and brass cut into the music. After an exact repeat of the taut opening dance down a tone in pitch, we cut to a section where wild, Dionysian forces are briefly unleashed: thundering in the low drums, thrashing orchestral unisons, whooping whole-tone-scale calls on brass and winds thrown around the orchestra in uninhibited counterpoint. Nijinsky has the girl at breaking point here, repeatedly collapsing, flailing, pounding the floor, rallying, dragging her exhausted leg in an attempt to walk.

The taut, opening dance makes an attempt to break into the Dionysian music but finally re-establishes itself for only the final minute of the piece. The Chosen One valiantly restarts her dance, but the music intensifies as the motivic cells repeat and repeat at closer intervals to each other, the whole orchestra coalesces on a repeating motive in percussive rhythmic unison, and the rate of activity in the drums and basses increases until there is no sonic space left. At this point the music breaks off. On an upward rush on the flutes, the Chosen One falls dead to the floor. On the final, downward crash, the tribesmen lift her body to the sky.

The Aftershocks

When *The Rite of Spring* was performed again in Paris less than a year after its catastrophic premiere, it was minus ballet, in a concert performance at the Casino de Paris on 5 April 1914. Pierre Monteux conducted but, otherwise, the occasion could not have been more different from the events of May 1913. The performance was a triumph, the audience listening in rapt silence and, by his own account, Stravinsky was carried out of the theatre on the shoulders of an adoring public, reporting Diaghilev's remark, 'Our little Igor now requires police escorts out of his concerts, like a prize fighter.' Diaghilev, Stravinsky added mischievously, 'was always verdantly envious of any success of mine outside of his Ballet'.[1] But the outbreak of the First World War hindered further performances and no printed score was published until 1921. Throughout the 1920s, *The Rite* gradually began to be performed more regularly in Europe and in the United States. In 1929, Pierre Monteux conducted the first commercial recording with the Orchestre Symphonique de Paris, closely followed by Stravinsky's own in the same year and, in 1930, the first US recording by Leopold Stokowski and the Philadelphia Orchestra appeared.

The piece was considered difficult for orchestras to play but, as the twentieth century progressed, it took its place as a staple of the repertoire. To date there have been as many as 165 commercial recordings. By the 1970s, skilled youth orchestras were beginning to perform it: in 1975 Pierre Boulez conducted the National Youth Orchestra of Great Britain and, in 1988, Leonard Bernstein said in a filmed rehearsal with the students of the Schleswig-Holstein Orchestra that what had once been practically unplayable has become 'the ideal kids' piece', clearly enjoying the fact that this piece about youth and renewal was now accessible to skilled young musicians. As *The Rite* became a fixture in concert halls, conductor and orchestras faced a new challenge: how could they avoid taming this dangerous beast? The conductor Esa-Pekka Salonen says:

> The actual mechanics of it are no longer a challenge: it's now more about how to make it sound difficult and risky again; outrageous, threatening and scary. It was on its way to becoming a flashy concert piece where orchestras strut their stuff. If ever there was a piece which doesn't deserve that fate, it's *The Rite of Spring*.[2]

Mirga Gražinytė-Tyla is another contemporary conductor who is determined *The Rite* should never become well behaved:

> It must *never* be normal. . . you have to find the raw open energy and incredible weight of the earth in the body. . . it has to be on the edge of classical music and noise.[3]

Stravinsky himself conducted *The Rite* many times and recorded it on three occasions. He was dismissive of the 'conductor's myth' that the constantly changing metres were a huge challenge: 'It's arduous but not difficult – the conductor is hardly more than a mechanical agent, a time beater who fires a pistol at the start of each section but lets the music run by itself.' He compared it to another piece from the same period, Alban Berg's Three Pieces for Orchestra which, he said, depended for its success on 'the conductor's nuances'.[4]

The conductor Marin Alsop supports Stravinsky's view:

> I try to find the right groove, the right swing for each section; it's an amazing feeling when you get a big group of people in the same rhythmic groove: after that, you don't have to do that much as a conductor.[5]

Vladimir Jurowski concurs that the conductor's main job in *The Rite* is to realize the very precise instructions that

Stravinsky laid out in the score, leaving little room for a subjective interpretation:

> In other pieces of the Romantic past you could put a layer of interpretation upon the music without damaging the core of the piece. In *The Rite of Spring*, the nature of the piece is that you need to lay it bare rather than add anything on the top.[6]

THE SHADOW OF THE RITE

It's impossible to imagine twentieth-century classical music without *The Rite of Spring*. It's everywhere, even if there are few composers who have dared take it on directly. Robert Craft, in his introduction to Stravinsky's sketches for *The Rite* describes its relationship to all the music that came after it as that of 'an ancestor, a prize bull that has inseminated the whole modern movement'. The direct homages tended to appear early in the life of *The Rite*. The twenty-two-year-old Prokofiev arrived in Paris in the summer of 1913 just too late to hear the premiere of *The Rite of Spring*, but he managed to get hold of a score. The following year Diaghilev met Prokofiev in London and, hoping that he had another Stravinsky on his hands, commissioned him to write a ballet for the Ballets Russes Paris season on pagan Russian themes. Diaghilev introduced him to the poet Sergey Gorodetsky and together they worked on a ballet entitled *Ala and Lolly*, based on stories and rituals of the ancient Scythians, the nomadic tribes that had inspired Roerich's scenario for *The Rite*. The pagan Russian theme of the new ballet, as well as the orgiastic dances, repetitive rhythms and dissonant harmonies are all clearly written in the shadow of *The Rite*. But Prokofiev's rhythms are regular, the dissonance always resolves and its clear originality is of a very different nature from its obvious model. Diaghilev rejected *Ala and Lolly* for being too conventional, not

Stravinsky at his conductor's stand.

modern enough for the Ballets Russes. Prokofiev refashioned the music into a concert piece that has enjoyed a successful life in the concert hall as the *Scythian Suite*.

Shortly after the thirty-three-year-old French composer Edgard Varèse arrived in New York in 1915, he began work on the giant orchestral piece *Amériques*, which bore striking similarities to Stravinsky's ballet with its brutal, heavy rhythm and relationship between music and noise. The piece is peppered with near-direct quotes from *The Rite*, starting from its opening sinuous flute melody, a close cousin of the solo bassoon passage at the start of *The Rite;* this is accompanied on harps by an ostinato pattern that uses exactly the same notes as the ticking ostinato from the 'Auguries of Spring' section of *The Rite. Amériques* has been described as an urban *Rite of Spring*, with sounds of New York's sirens, the clanking and grinding of overhead railways, river and road traffic all recognizable in the music. Varèse is more explicit than Stravinsky was in his depiction of a mechanized, twentieth-century world, but *Amériques* also shares with its predecessor a backdrop of prehistory: these Americas are ancient and mysterious as well as modern and industrial.

American composer George Antheil, the self-styled 'bad boy of music'[7] took the idea of machine music even further with his 1924 *Ballet mécanique** in which sirens, player-pianos and aeroplane propellers all appear in the orchestra. *The music of *Ballet mécanique* owes much to *The Rite* in its pounding, assymetrical dance rhythms and Cubist, cut-up structure. As with Varèse's *Amériques*, there are direct quotes of snatches of melody scattered throughout the score, and the opening takes us straight into what sounds like a pared-down version of the 'Dance of the

---

* The music was conceived originally to accompany Fernand Léger's Cubist art film of the same name.

Earth' from the end of Part 1 of *The Rite*. In post-revolutionary Russia, machine music took on a political significance. Alexander Mosolov's 1927 *Iron Foundry* was composed to celebrate steel production in the Soviet Union but is uncannily close to the polyrhythmic clamour of the 'Procession of the Sage' from Stravinsky's ancient rite.

As the twentieth century wore on, the innovations of *The Rite of Spring* in rhythm, orchestration and harmony became absorbed into new music, even if there were fewer explicit homages: it just made everything else possible. So, the notion that rhythm could be as important a feature of music as pitch became a liberating idea for composers from Varèse and György Ligeti to the American minimalists such as Steve Reich and, later, the industrial post-minimalism of Louis Andriessen, Michael Gordon and Julia Wolfe. The sound of *The Rite of Spring*, where music teeters on the edge of noise, must surely have influenced electronic pioneers such as Daphne Oram, Karlheinz Stockhausen and Iannis Xenakis. And, in the 1980s, Harrison Birtwistle wrote *Earth Dances* for large orchestra. With its shifting geological layers of orchestral textures and patterns, its music as well as the title are an explicit tribute to *The Rite of Spring*.

The ecstatic, opulent spirituality of the music of Olivier Messiaen could not be further in sound from the brutality of *The Rite of Spring*, but some of the most characteristic elements in Messiaen's compositional toolkit owe a big debt to Stravinsky's *Rite*: the daringly unpredictable rhythms made up of rhythmic cells of different sizes, and the cut-and-paste, Cubist approach to structure, where blocks of musical material sit next to each other without transition or connective tissue; these are signature Messiaen techniques, found in works such as *Turangalîla-Symphonie* and *Et exspecto resurrectionem mortuorum*, but they would not have been possible without *The Rite of Spring*. In-depth analysis of *The Rite* was an essential element of Messiaen's famous post-war Paris Conservatoire classes out of which emerged the giants of the European avant-garde, including Pierre Boulez, Karlheinz Stockhausen and Iannis Xenakis. Stravinsky's ballet score was, Messiaen believed, an essential text for an emerging composer. The British composer George Benjamin, who attended Messiaen's class as a teenager in the 1970s, says:

> Messiaen's analysis of *The Rite of Spring* made a very big impact on his students. It's behind a huge amount of his rhythmic and structural and orchestral thinking. Listen to the second movement of *Turangalîla* or the very end of the whole piece – these are toccatas for massive orchestra, full of accentuation. The sensibility is entirely different from *The Rite* but it would have been entirely impossible without it.

For Benjamin, composing in the twenty-first century, *The Rite* continues to resonate for him and his contemporaries:

> The rhythmical construction, the incredibly bold, novel way of making form; the harmonic innovation and the fantastic instinct for line, register and timbre – how to make instruments sound so brilliantly.

He backs up Robert Craft's idea that, going beyond its technical innovations, *The Rite of Spring* fired the starting pistol for the very idea of bold modernity in twentieth-century music:

> I suppose composers everywhere have been aware of this spectacular and glamorous scandal that happened in Paris and many have yearned to have a similar sort of impact. It's a very rare thing.[8]

There is a story that Stravinsky went with some friends to the New York jazz club Birdland one evening in 1951. Whispers went round that the great composer was in the house, seated at a table near the stage. When Charlie Parker came on with his quintet, he didn't acknowledge Stravinsky but launched straight into the ferociously fast bebop of 'Ko Ko', one of his most pyrotechnic numbers. When the second chorus came around, Parker seamlessly quoted *The Firebird* in his solo 'as if it had always been there', according to an eye witness – and then moved on as if it had never happened.[9] Stravinsky is reported to have been so delighted that he banged his glass on the table, causing its contents to spill on the people at the table behind. The story illustrates that Stravinsky and jazz musicians were comfortable around each other. They understood each other's language even if the composer once dismissed jazz as 'a kind of masturbation that never arrives anywhere'.[10] Stravinsky the kleptomaniac had appropriated ragtime rhythms in *The Soldier's Tale* and *Ragtime for Eleven Instruments* as early as 1918 and those syncopations had appeared in many works since. A few years before the Birdland incident, he had written a work for jazz performers, the *Ebony Concerto* (1945), for the clarinettist Woody Herman and his band.

Parker chose to quote *The Firebird* at Birdland, but it could just as easily have been *The Rite of Spring*: two years earlier in Paris, he'd acknowledged that he was in the hometown of *The Rite* by quoting the opening bassoon melody in his solo on 'Salt Peanuts'. Leonard Bernstein called *The Rite* 'prehistoric jazz' with good reason.[11] Jazz and *The Rite of Spring* came into being at almost exactly the same time, and the ballet has been an irresistible source for jazz musicians right up until the twenty-first century. No other piece of classical music makes so many appearances

in jazz, and it's not hard to see why. The orchestral stabs, jerks and slashes set against choruses of high winds in *The RIte of Spring* prefigure the texture of big-band music. The rhythmic layering and polyrhythms in *The Rite* foretell the complexity of bebop; sometimes it is hard to believe that *The Rite*'s rhythms do not have the same African sources as the giants of modern jazz. The octatonic, whole-tone and polytonal harmonies in *The RIte* became staples of modern jazz harmony, and the ostinato patterns that underpin almost everything in *The Rite* are close cousins of the jazz riff.

Parker's 'Salt Peanuts' solo seems to have started a trend for jazz musicians too numerous to list to use the opening bassoon melody, that Lithuanian folk tune, as a kind of *idée fixe*, a calling card to be thrown down in a solo. In Joni Mitchell's 'Talk to Me' from her 1977 album *Don Juan's Reckless Daughter* we hear the first phrase of *The Rite* melody before we hear Mitchell's voice. It floats high on the electric bass guitar played by Jaco Pastorius for whom those few notes were a musical signature that he frequently dropped into live and recorded performances. Pastorius's Stravinsky signature was also captured on Weather Report's *Heavy Weather* album where he slips the quote into his solo on the final track, 'Havona'. Going far beyond quotation, Ornette Coleman's 'Sleep Talking' on his 2005 album *Sound Grammar* extends the bassoon melody, giving it back something of its folk feel and using it as the basis for an extended composition. The Lithuanian wedding song has become a jazz standard.

Other jazz musicians took on larger chunks of *The Rite*. Alice Coltrane in her 1976 album *Eternity* is clearly attracted to the explicitly spiritual and mystic quality of the piece. Her track 'Spring Rounds' seems, at first, to be a straight arrangement of one of the few moments of calm in *The Rite*, the slow, heavy *khorovod* where the girls celebrate spring. And, in case anyone

Charlie Parker, Los Angeles, c.1945.

were to think that this is a female musician choosing the most 'feminine' moment of *The Rite of Spring*, Coltrane does not avoid the brief spasm of violence that happens towards the end of Stravinsky's original. She takes it to an even more shattering climax than Stravinsky does, letting the music veer wildly out of control before restoring it to its vernal calm.

In 2011, the Bad Plus, a jazz trio who had made their name with versions of songs by Radiohead, Bowie and Nirvana, among others, decided to take on the entire *Rite of Spring* with the greatly reduced forces of piano, bass and drums. 'We didn't want to be part of the tradition of jazz guys taking a little bit of it and soloing on it,' said the Bad Plus's drummer Dave King in a radio interview. 'We just wanted to know it and play it. . . to see how hard it could rock.'[12] The Bad Plus version is a faithful performance of the original music in its entirety, using Stravinsky's own piano-duet version as a starting point, the piano and bass re-creating the full score as much as possible. No one improvises apart from the drummer, who adds such sounds as are necessary to give a sense of the power and energy of the original. The result sounds like *The Rite of Spring*, but it also sounds like newly composed twenty-first-century jazz.

The uncategorizable Frank Zappa was a self-confessed Stravinsky obsessive and claimed to have listened to *The Rite of Spring* 'more than any man in the world'.[13] Stravinsky quotes are all over Zappa's music. 'In-A-Gadda-Stravinsky', a track on his 1988 *Guitar* album, Zappa becomes the latest in line to riff on *The Rite*'s opening bassoon melody in a guitar solo. Long before that, Zappa's 1967 Mothers of Invention album *Absolutely Free* is peppered with references to *The Rite* in both the music and the lyrics. One track is promisingly titled 'Invocation and Ritual Dance of the Young Pumpkin' but, perversely, quotes *The Planets* by Gustav Holst and includes not a note of Stravinsky.

The Rite of Spring, with its powerful riffs, extended harmonies and Scythian violence has been a trace element in the more adventurous corners of rock music, consciously or not, since the 1960s, from Zappa to King Crimson to Metallica. It even makes an appearance as a signifier for hedonistic abandon in 1990s pop: 'I feel like taking all my clothes off, dancing to *The Rite of Spring*,' sings Neil Tennant of the Pet Shop Boys in their 1993 single 'I Wouldn't Normally Do This Kind of Thing'. This is more than just a good rhyme: the cover art of the record shows a circle of young men in pink tops holding hands and dancing around a male Chosen One in a late-twentieth-century gay *khorovod*. Another confident reclamation of the territory of *The Rite* came in 2009 with the Russian folk metal band Arkona. The frontwoman and songwriter Maria Arkhipova is known as 'Masha Scream' for her

The American musician and composer Frank Zappa, 1972.

'death growl' vocal style and her song lyrics use ancient Slavic myths and stories. Her 2009 song 'Yarilo' is named after the sun god of *The Rite of Spring*. When Masha Scream performs the song, its folk-like melody accompanied by a mix of heavy metal and Russian folk instruments, she whirls round the stage cloaked in an animal skin, dressed as Roerich dressed the old men who sacrificed a young girl in the 1913 ballet. Masha is about as potent a symbol of female power as it is possible to get and, a century on, it seems that she is getting revenge.

Masha 'Scream' Arkhipova performing with Arkona, Budapest, 2014.

For generations of people, *The Rite of Spring* means dinosaurs. Even one of the most sophisticated musicians of the twentieth century, Leonard Bernstein, repeatedly refers to dinosaurs when talking about the work. That is because many of us first experienced the music in tandem with Walt Disney's prehistoric images from his 1940 animation feature *Fantasia*. *Fantasia* was Disney's attempt to bring the technical innovations that his studio had developed into the realm of high art, with new animations to classical music including Tchaikovsky's *Nutcracker* and Beethoven's 'Pastoral' Symphony. The film was also to have an educational aspect, with the Philadelphia Orchestra conducted by Leopold Stokowski in the studio and a narrator explaining the instruments of the orchestra and the physical nature of sound.

In 1939, Stravinsky signed a contract with Disney for US$6,000,* which was much needed income at a time when the outbreak of the Second World War in Europe forced the second major uprooting of his life, from France to the USA, and dried up his income from performances.[14] Perhaps it is for that reason that Stravinsky agreed terms that allowed Disney complete freedom to chop up and edit the music of *The Rite* as he wished, and to associate it with any imags that he chose.

Disney did indeed make free with the structure of *The Rite* for his dinosaur ballet. He cut over a third of the music completely, and reordered what was left. To Stravinsky's particular dismay, the final 'Sacrificial Dance' did not make the cut, nor did the 'Spring Rounds' or the 'Ritual of the Rival Tribes'. The 'Dance of the Earth' was excised from the first half of the ballet and moved

---

*   At the time of writing, this is the equivalent of US$105,000.

overleaf
A still from the *Rite of Spring* segment
of Walt Disney's *Fantasia*.

to near the end and, in the most surprising cut of all, the opening bassoon melody appears at the end as a brief coda in a very un-*Rite of Spring*-like symmetry.

But Disney's courage in choosing a work that was only twenty-six years old was matched by the ambition that he had for his new version of it. This was not to be an ancient Slavic ritual but an attempt at a scientifically accurate depiction of the beginnings of life on earth. 'Science, not art, wrote the scenario for this film,' says the narrator, and Disney had, indeed, consulted with leading scientists, including the biologist Julian Huxley and the astronomer Edwin Hubble. The 'Introduction' to the ballet depicts deep space, vast nothingness, galaxies and shooting stars. The violent accents in 'The Augurs of Spring' are choreographed by perfectly timed volcanic explosions. The opening of Part 2 depicts the beginnings of life on earth with cells dividing, meeting and multiplying, as foretold in Jacques Rivière's 'biological ballet' comment in his 1913 review; the violence of the 'Glorification of the Chosen One' section depicts the fatal fight of the dinosaurs and, appropriately, the 'Dance of the Earth' is accompanied by images of catastrophic earthquakes that force mountains up from out of the earth. Although Disney chose an entirely different scenario from the original ballet, his dinosaurs are walking through prehistoric landscapes that, with their muted colours, are uncannily close to Roerich's backdrops from 1913, almost as if the Disney colourists had used the peasant vegetable dyes beloved of the Russian folk revival movement.

Stravinsky settled in Hollywood in 1940 and lived there for most of the rest of his life. He hoped that writing film scores would supplement his income but, although he composed music for several film projects, the specific demands of the studios meant that none of it ended up being heard in the cinema. He repurposed much of it for concert works; for example, the music that he wrote for *The Song of Bernadette* (1943)* became the middle movement of his *Symphony in Three Movements* (1946). However, in another sense, Stravinsky did become a film composer in that the sound of his music resonates in film scores right up to the present day. *The Rite of Spring* in particular became a source book for which movie composers have reached when summoning up primitivism, suspense, violence, threat or mystery. Just like in jazz, the borrowings from and homages to *The Rite of Spring* in film music are too numerous to begin to list.

While so much film music is infused with essence of *The Rite of Spring* in a general way, some film composers were more explicit in their homages. The percussive jabs from the shower scene in Bernard Herrmann's score for Hitchcock's *Psycho* (1960) owe much to the repetitive orchestral violence of *The Rite* and Elmer Bernstein, in his 1962 score for *To Kill a Mockingbird*, accompanies a sequence showing an attack on children by the rhythmic jabs akin to the 'Sacrificial Dance'. The *Mockingbird* score is suffused with references to *The Rite* throughout, but the cue that underscores the lynch mob in *Mockingbird* is remarkable, like a mini *Rite of Spring* in under three minutes: it opens with a floating, high bassoon melody, joined by a rhythmically free clarinet, just as in Stravinsky's Part 1 'Introduction'. Slow stamping rhythms hint at 'The Auguries of Spring', a high flute folk tune at the 'Spring Rounds'; rocking winds chords indicate the 'Introduction' to Part 2, followed by the unmistakable slow trudge and low trumpets of the 'Ritual Action of the Ancestors'. Stravinsky might or might not have seen this film but he was known to bemoan what he perceived as the overuse in the movies of versions of this 'Ritual Action' music as a ubiquitous signal of approaching threat.

---

* The film was eventually scored by Alfred Newman, who won an Academy Award for it.

Jerry Goldsmith summons up *The Rite* to score primitivism and violence in his music for *Planet of the Apes* (1968). As with *To Kill a Mockingbird*, there are references throughout the score, most explicitly in the central scene where apes on horseback are hunting primitive humans in the long grass, where we hear unmistakable references to the chase music and hunting calls of the 'Ritual of Abduction' as well as the fight music of the 'Ritual of the Rival Tribes'.

But it is the film composer John Williams who has most thoroughly mined *The Rite of Spring* in his soundtracks. Williams wears his knowledge of twentieth-century orchestral music on his sleeve, from Holst to Bartók to Korngold, but *The Rite of Spring* has remained a fixed point to which he has constantly returned to pay homage. The leitmotif that signals the approaching shark in Spielberg's 1975 film *Jaws* has become arguably the most famous few seconds of music in cinema history. The growling double-basses building up to stamping rhythms of thickly dissonant chords, slashed into by loud accents at unpredictable intervals are echoes of 'The Augurs of Spring'. Throughout the *Star Wars* films, Williams has returned to the home territory of *The Rite*. In the music for the 'Dune Sea of Tatooine' sequence in the original 1977 *Star Wars* can be heard echoes of the rocking chords of the 'Introduction' to Part 2, which then cut to a clear suggestion of the 'Ritual Action of the Ancestors' and the high tuba tune of 'Procession of the Sage'. The influence of *The Rite* is still apparent in the 2015 *Star Wars: The Force Awakens*, where the Rahtar attack is scored by music that clearly echoes the 'Sacrificial Dance'. And the frantic gestures of the 'Glorification of the Chosen One' are reproduced in the climactic scene of *Jurassic Park* (1993): John WIlliams has returned *The Rite* to the dinosaurs.

For decades after the 1913 premiere, new choreographic versions of *The Rite of Spring* were few and far between. Stravinsky could have been forgiven for thinking that he had got his way: *The Rite* was an abstract concert work and had shaken off its roots in dance. It was not until the mid-twentieth century, when the composer was an old man, that significant re-stagings began to appear. Since that time the steady stream of new dance versions has become a torrent. The centenary celebrations in 2013 encouraged even more and it seems to be almost a requirement for twenty-first-century choreographers that they square up to the beast as their own rite of passage. Choreographic versions can now be counted in their hundreds, from solo performances to massed participation stagings, from African dance interpretations to immersive digital experiences.

The first new choreography came in 1920, seven years after the Nijinsky premiere, with the Ballets Russes. If Stravinsky was determined that *The Rite of Spring*'s place was in the concert hall and not on the stage, Diaghilev was equally determined to restore its fortunes as a ballet. He commissioned Leonid Massine, who had stepped into Nijinsky's shoes as the Ballets Russes choreographer and Diaghilev's lover, to make a new version: at least, the steps would be new, but the set and costumes were Roerich's originals and, to stage the premiere, they returned to the scene of the crime at the Théâtre des Champs-Élysées. Stravinsky accepted Massine's 1920 version partly because it largely did away with any story, but also because of its relationship to the music: Nijinsky's had been, he thought, a too literal, moment-by-moment choreography, a step for every single beat in the score. Massine's choreography had a more fluid approach, freely connecting and bridging key points in the music. As Lydia Sokolova, who was Massine's Chosen One in 1920, wrote: 'I danced, I met the orchestra precisely at the two

overleaf
A photograph from the 1995 performance of *The Rite of Spring*
choreographed by Pina Bausch in 1975.

places that I should, and we finished together.'[15] But Massine must have felt that he had fallen victim to the curse of *The Rite*: in a rerun of the Nijinsky affair, Massine was summarily sacked from the company shortly after his *Rite* had been staged, allegedly because of his relationship with company dancer Vera Savina. In an ugly incident uncomfortably close to the world of *The Rite of Spring*, Diaghilev is reported to have got Savina drunk, stripped her naked and thrown her at Massine, in a hotel room, declaring, 'Behold your ideal beauty!'[16]

The Rite of Spring is a story of the sacrifice of a young woman dreamt up by three men: Stravinsky, Roerich and Nijnsky. It took many years for female choreographers to tackle it but, once they did, some of the most triumphant choreographies of this problematic narrative have been by women: Martha Graham, Pina Bausch, Sascha Waltz among them. One of the first significant post-Ballets Russes versions was made in 1957 for the Städtische Oper Berlin by the then seventy-year-old German choreographer Mary Wigman, who had been a pioneer of modern and Expressionist dance in Weimar Germany. Like Nijinsky's, this choreography was subsequently lost, but was reconstructed from diaries, notes and photographs in the centenary year of 2013. Wigman's *Sacre du printemps* has been described as a feminist *Rite*, the stage dominated much of the time by three priestess-like figures, and we see the community coming under the spell of the male Sage figure who initiates the sacrifice. The fear of the girl victim is highly controlled and stylized – she spends long periods in the 'Sacrificial Dance' barely moving at all. But the ending, even in a feminist *Rite of Spring*, is the same: the girl dies.

The Rite continued to force artists to imagine the future. In 1959, at the dawn of the 1960s, French choreographer Maurice Béjart made sex the focus of his *Sacre du printemps*, first performed at the Théâtre Royal de la Monnaie in Brussels. For the entire first half of his ballet, men in flesh-coloured bodysuits perform high-testosterone animalistic dances to prepare a chosen man for sexual union with one of the women. The ritual sacrifice is not a dance to the death but the sex act. The first British *Rite of Spring*, for the Royal Ballet, followed soon after, in 1962, when choreographer Kenneth MacMillan invited Australian painter Sidney Nolan to design sets and costumes evoking the primitivism of the original in an Australian outback setting. Nolan's backdrop for Part 2 was a giant sun with a stem at the bottom: a mushroom cloud in this the most dangerous year of the Cold War.

'How would you feel if you had to dance knowing you had to die?'[17] is the question that Pina Bausch asked her Tanztheater Wuppertal dancers when making her 1975 *Sacre* which is still, four decades later, a vital and terrifying staging. If other choreographers have stylized – and distanced us from – the fear in *The Rite*, Bausch makes it very real right from the beginning of the work, which is performed on a stage covered in soil. A blood-red cloth is ever present, passed around the women partly in terror, partly in fascination; at the end, it becomes the red dress in which the Chosen One dances herself to death. The obsessive, repetitive movements of her 'Sacrificial Dance' are foretold by all of the women right from the start of the piece: the terrible end is known at the beginning. The Bausch *Sacre* puts gender at the heart of the work: the rival tribes are men against women; the repetitive, machine-like dancing of the women emphasizes their female bodies: repeatedly grabbing their wombs or striking their breasts, bowing down towards their genitalia or pulling up their dresses like little girls, all in a manner that goes far beyond the eroticism of Béjart. These women, and the men, are real and they end up covered in soil, in sweat and panting for breath.

All this time, the lost Nijinsky choreography was a memory kept alive by anecdote, press reviews and in the memoirs of some of the key players. In Los Angeles in 1987 the Joffrey Ballet performed a reconstruction of the original Nijinsky–Roerich

overleaf
A photograph from Klaus Obermaier's version
of *The Rite of Spring*, 2007.

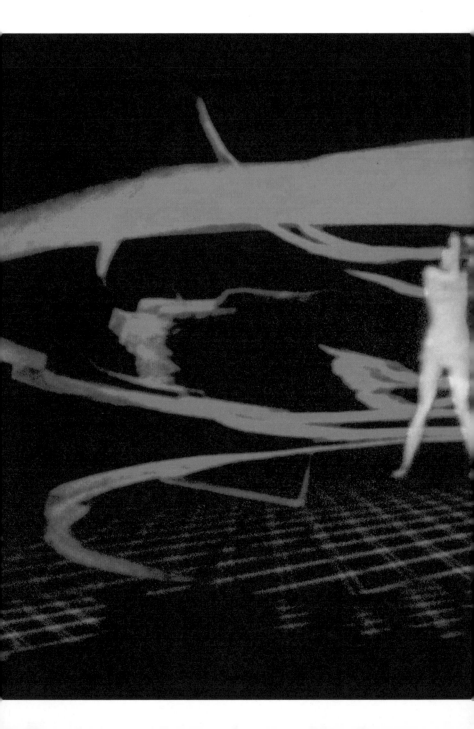

production created by Millicent Hodson and Kenneth Archer after painstaking study of these contemporary sources. There were only three surviving photographs, but there were also drawings by Roerich and sketches made in rehearsals by Valentine Gross that captured the dancers' positions and movements. Stravinsky had published some notes on the choreography in 1969 along with the *Rite of Spring* sketches and in 1967 Marie Rambert came across a piano score from 1913 annotated with her own detailed notes of Nijinsky's instructions to the dancers. The reconstruction reveals something of what contemporary accounts tell us. We see in the flesh the novelty of the awkward 'anti-ballet' body shapes. We see a ballet of seething massed energy in counterpoint with the isolation of the individuals within it: Jacques Rivière's 1913 eye-witness account of a 'biological ballet' with cells splitting and multiplying and spinning off becomes real on the stage. We also see for real the mechanical tragedy of the final dance to the death. Hodson's and Archer's reconstruction has been performed all over the world and was brought to the Théâtre des Champs-Élysées on 29 May 2013, a hundred years to the day since the riotous premiere, where it was performed alongside a new version

by German choreographer Sascha Waltz. It also formed the basis of a 2005 BBC film that dramatized the first night in 1913.[18]

The seething, massed energy and community action of *The Rite* provoked British choreographer Royston Maldoom to create a dance involving large numbers of untrained teenagers in communities from Addis Ababa to New York to Berlin; in the Berlin version in 2003, 250 young performers were on stage with the Berlin Philharmonic and Simon Rattle.

At the opposite extreme, many choreographers have been tempted to distil the energy of *The Rite* down to a single performer: Molissa Fenley, Meryl Tankard and Tero Saarinen have all created solo versions, Saarinen's involving images of his dancing self projected on to his body. A recent, striking solo version of *The Rite of Spring* by the so-called Mother of African Contemporary Dance, the Senegalese Germaine Acogny and choreographer Olivier Dubois expressed the violence of *The Rite* in terms of the brutality of colonialism. *Mon Élue Noire* (My Black Chosen One) sees Acogny, in her seventies, alone on a black stage, smoking a pipe, dancing to Stravinsky's music, singing over it and reciting texts from Aimé Césaire's 'Discourse on Colonialism' which describes how, in treating the colonized as savages, the colonizers themselves become savage. Acogny describes how, in being inside the ancient rituals of Stravinsky's *Rite*, she is honouring her grandmother, a Yoruba priestess. The Austrian digital artist Klaus Obermaier created a solo version in which members of the audience wear 3D glasses and the dancer's movements are captured by multiple video cameras and then morphed, fragmented, multiplied and projected into the theatre in real time as she dances, filling the entire theatre with ballets of disembodied limbs or snowstorms of the dancer's curled body.

But some choreographers have taken an oblique view of *The Rite*. When Akram Khan was invited by Sadler's Wells in London to create a project to celebrate the 2013 centenary, he

Germaine Acogny performing *Mon Élue Noire*, 2018.

felt that he could not tackle it directly, convinced that he could never equal the Pina Bausch version: 'When I hear the music, all I can see is her work.' Instead Khan created, in collaboration with contemporary musicians Nitin Sawhney, Jocelyn Pook and Ben Frost, a work entitled *iTMOi – In the Mind of Igor* – that explored the idea of sacrifice and the preoccupations and attributes of Stravinsky, including the assymetrical rhythms, folk music, orthodox chant and even his tendency to be economical with the truth: the idea that Stravinsky had spent his long life lying about *The Rite of Spring* inspired Khan and his team to explore masks, the changing of stories, different versions of reality.[19]

Another oblique approach is that of the British choreographer and sculptor Florence Peake, whose 2017 installation *Rite*, displayed in a gallery in east London, goes into combat with the idea of the great masterwork. In one room of the gallery is a video of the dancer Rosemary Lee buried in a bed of wet clay and moving to what she can remember of the music of *The Rite of Spring*, gradually emerging from the mud and, at the end, being sucked back into it. We hear fragments of Stravinsky occasionally from another room but the dancer on the video can only hear it in her head. Like Pina Bausch, Peake is concerned with the relationship of the human body to the earth and to oppression and fear. In yet another room in the gallery, the clay in which the remembered *Rite of Spring* has been danced by Rosemary Lee has been dried, cut up into tiles, glazed, fired and then displayed together, the imprint of the struggle of the woman still visible but fragmented, like the Sacrificial Dance of the Chosen One, the victim of this tragedy.

Perhaps it seems odd to describe *The Rite of Spring* as a tragedy. Stravinsky, after all, said, 'There are simply no regions for soul searching in *The Rite of Spring*.'[20] For all its visceral power and, yes, emotional impact, commentators from Jacques Rivière to Richard Taruskin have insisted that there is no individual romantic feeling in the work. What makes *The Rite of Spring* so shockingly modern is that its savagery and violence is mechanical, detached, dehumanized, foretelling the mass slaughter that became possible in the twentieth century. *The Rite of Spring* reaches back into a deep past to predict a terrifying world to come. Writing soon after the first performance of the ballet in 1913, Jacques Rivière wrote:

> We witness the movements of man at a time when he did not yet exist as an individual. . . At no time during her dance does the Chosen Maiden betray the personal terror that ought to fill her soul. She accomplishes a rite; she is absorbed by a social function and, without giving any sign of comprehension or interpretation, she acts according to the will and the convulsions of a being more vast than she, a monster full of ignorance and appetites, cruelty and gloom.[21]

And yet. . . The artists who continue, in ever increasing droves, to tackle *The Rite of Spring*, from Pina Bausch to Florence Peake, have looked to find the humanity and emotional truth in it, to challenge the idea that the killing of an innocent girl can ever be merely a device for a work of art. Nijinsky himself knew this when he made the very first dance for *The Rite of Spring* in 1913. Both Marie Rambert and Bronislawa Nijinska, who witnessed him rehearsing 'The Chosen One' in the rehearsal studio, remembered that the emotional impact of the original 'Sacrificial Dance' was devastating. When Nijinsky demonstrated the movement to Maria Piltz it was, wrote Rambert, 'the greatest tragic dance I have ever seen'.[22] And, I firmly believe, that whether it is danced or played in the concert hall *The Rite of Spring* remains, as its first choreographer Nijinsky intended, 'for an ordinary audience member a jolting impression and an emotional experience'.[23]

Some Recordings
(and one DVD) of *The Rite of Spring*

1958
Leonard Bernstein and the New York
Philharmonic; Sony, re-released 2013.
Recorded in a single session by one of
The Rite's most eloquent advocates;
Stravinsky himself was said to have been
impressed.

1959
Igor Markevitch with the Philharmonia
Orchestra; EMI. An early stereo recording
from a conductor who had been favoured
by Diaghilev.

1960
The seventy-eight-year-old Stravinsky
conducts *Le Sacre du Printemps*; Columbia
Symphony Orchestra, 1960, Columbia/CBS:
Sony CD (2013). A chance to hear what the
composer himself intended.

1969
Pierre Boulez, Cleveland Orchestra; Sony.
Boulez had analysed the work in detail and
it shows in this crisp, powerful recording.

1981
Antal Dorati and the Detroit Symphony
Orchestra; Decca. The first digital recording
and winner of the Grand Prix du Disque.

2013
Francois-Xavier Roth conducts his orchestra
Les Siècles playing instruments as close as
possible to those that would have been used
in 1913.

2015
Teodor Currentzis, MusicAeterna; Sony.
An orchestra hailing from Perm near the
Ural Mountains, led by a young Greek-
born conductor in a thrilling and fast
performance.

2009
Stravinsky and the Ballets Russes: *The
Firebird* and *The Rite of Spring*, Marinsky
Orchestra and Ballet, conducted by Valery
Gergiev. Millicent Hodson's reconstruction
of Nijinsky's original choreography on DVD,
Bel Air.

Further Reading

Jonathan Cross: *Critical Lives: Igor Stravinsky* (London: Reaktion Books, 2015).
An approachable and well-paced short biography of Stravinsky by the authoritative voice of the Professor of Musicology at the University of Oxford.

Peter Hill: *Stravinsky: The Rite of Spring. Cambridge Music Handbooks* (Cambridge: Cambridge University Press, 2000).
A valuable introduction to The Rite of Spring *with musical examples, analysis and historical context.*

Richard Taruskin: *Stravinsky and the Russian Traditions: A Biography of the Works Through* Mavra (Oxford: Oxford University Press, 1996).
Breathtaking scholarship in two volumes detailing the influence of Russian folk traditions on Stravinsky's early works.

Stephen Walsh: *Igor Stravinsky, a Creative Spring, Russia and France 1812–1934* and *Igor Stravinsky, the Second Exile, France and America 1934–1971* (London: Jonathan Cape, 1999 and 2006).
Authoritative and highly readable two-volume account of Stravinsky's long life by a leading Stravinsky scholar.

Severine Neff, Maureen Carr and Gretchen Horlacher (eds), Stephen Walsh (Foreword), *The Rite of Spring at 100* (Indiana University Press, 2017).
A series of international scholarly articles on many aspects of The Rite of Spring, *written in celebration of its centenary.*

Acknowledgements

I am grateful to the following people who were interviewed for this book:

Mirga Gražinytė-Tyla; Marin Alsop; Vladimir Jurowski; Esa-Pekka Salonen; George Benjamin; Millicent Hodson; Kenneth Archer; Deborah Bull; Meryl Tankard; Florence Peake.

Additional thanks to: Janis Susskind of Boosey and Hawkes, Paul Hoskins and Emma Brignall of Rambert Dance Company, Jeremy Peyton-Jones and Goldsmiths' College, Jonathan Cross, Sarah Alexander, Musicians of the National Youth Orchestra of Great Britain, Thomas Ades, Humphrey Burton, Jonny Greenwood, Jude Kelly, Bob Lockyer, Bruce Nockles, Jonathan Freeman Attwood and Kathryn Adamson of the Royal Academy of Music.

Notes

INTRODUCTION

1 Robert Craft, *Stravinsky: Chronicle of a Friendship*, 2nd rev. edn (Nashville and London: Vanderbilt University Press, 1994), p. 285.

2 Julian Street, 'Why I Became a Cubist', *Everybody's Magazine* 28 (June 1913).

3 From a 'London Letter' in the *Dial*, October 1921.

4 *Portraits of a Lifetime*, ed. and trans. Walter Clement (London: J. M. Dent & Sons, 1937), pp. 259–60.

5 Nijinsky, letter to Stravinsky, 25 January 1913, quoted in *Stravinsky in Pictures and Documents*, Vera Stravinsky and Robert Craft (New York: Simon and Schuster, 1978) p. 94.

1   WHO WAS IGOR STRAVINSKY?

1 Reproduced in Igor Stravinsky and Robert Craft, *Expositions and Developments* (London: Faber and Faber, 1962), pp. 14, 15.

2 Interview with the author, July 2017.

3 Igor Stravinsky and Robert Craft, *Memories and Commentaries* (London: Faber and Faber, 1960), p. 26.

4 Igor Stravinsky, *Chronicle of My Life* (London: Victor Gollancz, 1936).

5 Ibid.

2   THE REINVENTION OF THE RUSSIAN SOUL

1 Interview with Igor Stravinsky, *Komsomol'skaya Pravda*, 27 September 1962, quoted in Stephen Walsh, *Stravinsky*, vol. 2: *The Second Exile: France and America 1934–1971* (London: Jonathan Cape, 2006), p. 463.

2 Leo Tolstoy, *War and Peace*, Book 1, Chapter 5 (Cambridge World Classics, Kindle Edition).

3 Quoted in Marina Frolova-Walker, *Russian Music and Nationalism from Glinka to Stalin* (New Haven and London: Yale University Press, 2007), p. 52.

4 Jacques-Émile Blanche, 'Un Bilan artistique de Paris 1913', in *La Revue de Paris*, 1 December 1913, quoted in Truman Campbell Bullard, *The First Performance of Igor Stravinsky's 'Sacre du printemps'*, PhD diss., University of Rochester, 1971.

5 Quoted in Richard Taruskin, *Stravinsky and the Russian Traditions: A Biography of the Works through Mavra* (Oxford: Oxford University Press, 1996), Vol. 1, p. 523.

6 Alexandre Benois, *Reminiscences of the Russian Ballet* (London: Puttnam, 1941), quoted in Taruskin, *Stravinsky and the Russian Traditions: A Biography of the Works through* Mavra (Oxford: Oxford University Press, 1996), p. 535.

7 Serge Lifar, *Serge Diaghilev: His Life, His Work, His Legend, an Intimate Biography* [1940] (New York: Da Capo, 1976).

8 Jacques Rivière, 'Le Sacre du printemps', *Nouvelle revue française*, November 1913, pp. 706–30.

9 Victor Ilyitch Seroff, *The Real Isadora* (New York: Dial Press, 1971).

---

3 FROM A DREAM TO A FIRST NIGHT: THE MAKING OF THE RITE OF SPRING

1 Stravinsky, *Chronicle of My Life.*

2 Richard Taruskin, 'Resisting *The Rite*', in *Russian Music at Home and Abroad: New Essays* (Oakland, CA: University of California Press, 2016), p. 415.

3 Quoted in Taruskin, *Stravinsky and the Russian Traditions*, p. 864.

4 Letter 2 (15) December 1912, quoted in the supplement to Igor Stravinsky, *The Rite of Spring: Sketches 1911–1913: Facsimile Reproductions from the Autographs* (London: Boosey and Hawkes, 1969), p. 32.

5 Quoted in Jacqueline Decter, *Nicholas Roerich: The Life and Art of a Russian Master* (London: Thames and Hudson, 1989), p. 47.

6 Igor Stravinsky and Robert Craft, *Dialogues and a Diary* (Berkeley, CA: University of California Press, 1982), p. 90.

7 Nicholas Roerich, 'Joy in Art', in *Collected Works*, Book 1 (Moscow, 1914), quoted in Paul Griffiths and Edmund Griffiths, 'The Shaman, the Sage and the Sacrificial Victim – and Nicholas Roerich's Part in It All', in Hermann Danuser and Heidy Zimmermann (eds), *Avatar of Modernity: The Rite of Spring Reconsidered*, 3 vols (London: Boosey and Hawkes, 2013), p. 42.

8 Stephen Walsh explores this idea in *Igor Stravinsky, a Creative Spring, Russia and France 1812–1934* (London: Jonathan Cape, 1999), p. 170.

9 Quoted in *Bronislava Nijinska: Early Memoirs*, edited and translated by Irina Nijinska, and Jean Rawlinson, introduction by Anna Kisselgoff (New York: Holt, Rinehart and Winston, 1981), p. 448.

10 Letter, 19 June 1910, quoted in Igor Stravinsky, *The Rite of Spring: Sketches 1911–1913*, p. 27.

11 Letter, 27 July 1910, quoted in ibid, p. 29.

12 Letter, Stravinsky to Benois, 3 November 1910, quoted in Hermann Danuser and Heidy Zimmermann (eds), *Avatar of Modernity: The Rite of Spring Reconsidered* (London: Boosey and Hawkes, 2013), p. 444.

16 Gustav Linor, 'Au Théâtre des Champs-Élysées: *Le Sacre du printemps*', *Comœdia*, 30 May 1913; quoted in Bullard, *The First Performance of Igor Stravinsky's 'Sacre du printemps'*.

17 Lynn Garafola, *Diaghilev's Ballets Russes* (New York: Da Capo, 1989), p. 64.

18 From a 1951 radio interview, quoted in Kelly, *First Nights*, p. 325.

19 Sokolova, *Dancing for Diaghilev*, p. 44.

20 Robert Craft and Igor Stravinsky, *Conversations with Igor Stravinsky* (London: Faber and Faber, 1959), p. 46.

21 Igor Stravinsky remembers making this comment in the documentary CBS News Special: *Stravinsky* (TV); producer, writer David Oppenheim, first broadcast 3 May 1966.

22 Craft and Stravinsky, *Conversations*, p. 46.

23 Bronislava Nijinska, *Early Memoirs*, pp. 469–70.

24 Reported by Nijinska in *Early Memoirs* (p. 470), and others.

25 Victor Debay, 'Les Ballets Russes au Théâtre des Champs-Élysées', in *Le Courier musicale*, 15 June 1913, quoted in Bullard, *The First Performance of Igor Stravinsky's 'Sacre du printemps'*.

26 Doris Monteux, *It's All in the Music: The Life and Work of Pierre Monteux* (London: William Kimber and Co., 1965), p. 92.

27 Estaban Buch, 'The Scandal at Le Sacre: Games of Distinction and Dreams of Barbarism', in Danuser and Zimmermann (eds), *Avatar of Modernity*, p. 59.

28 Millicent Hodson, 'Death by Dancing in Nijinsky's *Rite*', in Severine Neff, Maureen Carr and Gretchen Horlacher (eds), *The Rite of Spring at 100* (Indiana University Press, 2017), p. 63.

29 Jacques Rivière, '*Le Sacre du printemps*', *Nouvelle revue française*, November 1913, pp. 706–30. Translated in Bullard, *The First Performance of Igor Stravinsky's 'Sacre du printemps'*.

30 Pierre Lalo, 'Théâtre des Champs-Élysées', *Le Temps*, 3 June 1913; quoted in Bullard, *The First Performance of Igor Stravinsky's 'Sacre du printemps'*.

31 See Rambert, *Quicksilver*, p. 64.

32 Carl Van Vechten, *Music After the Great War* (New York: Schirmer, 1915), pp. 87–8; quoted in Kelly, *First Nights*, p. 323.

33 Romola Nijinsky, *Nijinsky*, p. 167.

34 D. Monteux, *It's All in the Music*, p. 92.

35 Sokolova, *Dancing for Diaghilev*, p. 44.

36 Rambert, *Quicksilver*, p. 65.

37 Cocteau, *Cock and Harlequin*; quoted in Kelly, *First Nights*, p. 326.

38 Craft and Stravinsky, *Conversations*, pp. 46–7.

39 Florent Schmitt, 'Les Sacres [*sic*] du printemps de M. Igor Stravinsky', *Le Temps*, 4 June 1913; quoted in Bullard, *The First Performance of Igor Stravinsky's 'Sacre du printemps'*.

40 Octave Maus, *L'Art moderne*, 1 June 1913, quoted in Bullard, *The First Performance*.

41 Georges Pioch, 'Théâtre des Champs-Élysées', *Gil Blas*, 4 June 1913, quoted in Bullard, *The First Performance*.

42 Igor Stravinsky, Henri Postel du Mas, 'Un entretien avec M. Stravinsky', *Gil Blas*, 4 June 1913.

43 Jacques Rivière, '*Le Sacre du printemps*', *Nouvelle revue française*, 1 August 1913, pp. 309–13.

44 Jacques-Émile Blanche, 'Un Bilan Artistique'; quoted in Bullard, *The First Performance*.

5   THE MUSIC OF THE RITE OF SPRING: WHAT WAS SO NEW?

1   *Boston Herald*, February 1924; quoted in Nicolas Slonimsky, *Music Since 1900* (New York: Schirmer Books, 1994), p. 1016.

2   Stravinsky and Craft, *Memories and Commentaries*, p. 30.

3   Stravinsky and Craft, *Expositions and Developments*, pp. 147–8.

4   Interview with the author, September 2018.

5   Interview with the author, June 2017.

6   Leonard Bernstein, 'The Unanswered Question': *Six Talks at Harvard* (Cambridge, MA.: Harvard University Press, paperback edition 1981), p. 357.

7   Lalo, 'Théâtre des Champs-Élysées', quoted in Bullard, *The First Performance*.

8   Olivier Messiaen, trans. John Satterfield, *Technique of My Musical Language* (Paris: A. Leduc, 1956).

9   Letter to Findeizen, 15 December 1912, quoted in the supplement to *The Rite of Spring: Sketches 1911–1913*, p. 32.

6   THE RITE STEP BY STEP: A LISTENING GUIDE

1   Stravinsky and Craft, *Expositions and Developments*, p. 141.

2   Émile Vuillermoz, 'La Saison russe', translated in Bullard, *The First Performance*, and quoted in Hodson, 'Death by Dancing in Stravinsky's *Rite*', p. 58.

3   Lawrence Morton, 'Footnotes to Stravinsky Studies: *Le Sacre du printemps*', *Tempo* 128 (March 1979): pp. 9–16.

7   THE AFTERSHOCKS

1   Stravinsky and Craft, *Expositions and Developments*, p. 144.

2   Interview with the author, June 2017.

3   Interview with the author, July 2017.

4   Stravinsky and Craft, *Expositions and Developments*, p. 145.

5   Interview with the author, March 2017.

6   Interview with the author, July 2017.

7   *Bad Boy of Music* is the title of Antheil's autobiography (New York: Doubleday, 1945).

8   Interview with the author, September 2018.

9   See Alfred Appel, *Jazz Modernism: From Ellington and Armstrong to Matisse and Joyce* (New York: Knopf, 2002), p. 60.

10   Craft and Stravinsky, *Conversations*, p. 116.

11   Interview on Classical MPR Radio, 19 May 2011.

12   Rip Rense, 'A unique musical force or blasphemous freak: Which is Frank Zappa?', *Valley News* (Van Nuys, CA), 27 June 1976; quoted in researchblog. andremount.net, February 2010.

13   See Walsh, *Stravinsky: The Second Exile*, pp. 89–90.

14   Sokolova, *Dancing for Diaghilev*, pp. 162–3.

15   Quoted in Sjeng Scheijen, *Diaghilev: A Life* (London: Profile Books, 2010), p. 363.

16   Pina Bausch in the film *Pina* (2011), directed by Wim Wenders.

17   *Riot at the Rite* (BBC, 2005), written by Kevin Elyot and directed by Andy Wilson.

18   *iTMOi/Akram Khan Company – making of* (video), Sadler's Wells, London.

19   Igor Stravinsky and Robert Craft, *Dialogues and a Diary* (Berkeley: University of California Press, 1982), p. 90.

20   Rivière, '*Le Sacre du printemps*'.

21   Rambert, *Quicksilver*, p. 64.

22   Nijinsky letter to Stravinsky, 25 January 1913, quoted in *Stravinsky in Pictures and Documents*, p. 94.

Picture credits

pp.4–5 Johan Persson/Royal Opera House/ArenaPAL; p.11 Keystone/Getty Images; pp.20–1 AKG-images/Album; p.25 Sputnik/Bridgeman Images; p.26 Lebrecht Music & Arts/Alamy Stock Photo; p.29 State Russian Museum, St. Petersburg, Russia/Bridgeman Images; pp.38–9 Krassotkin, from Wikimedia Commons; p.41 DEA Picture Library/Getty Images; pp.45–46 Ilya Repin, from Wikimedia Commons; p.48 Cooper Hewitt, Smithsonian Design Museum, from Wikimedia Commons; pp.52–3 Chronicle/Alamy Stock Photo; p.54 Private Collection/Bridgeman Images; p.56 Universal Images Group/Getty; p.61 Keystone-France/Getty; pp.74–5 Pictorial Press Ltd/Alamy Stock Photo; pp.78–9 Private Collection/Bridgeman Images; p.85 Sasha/Stringer/Getty; pp.94–5 Antoine Bourdelle, from Wikimedia Commons; p.101 Lebrecht Music Arts/Bridgeman Images; pp.104–5 Getty Images/colourised by Marina Amaral; p.106 Lebrecht Music Arts/Bridgeman Images; p.109 Heritage Images/Getty; p.112 E.O.Hoppe/Stringer/Getty; pp.128–9 Igor Stravinsky Collection, Paul Sacher Foundation, Basel; pp.146–9 Ashmolean Museum, University of Oxford/Bridgeman Images; p.157 Roger-Viollet/TopFoto; p.164 Print Collector/Getty; p.170 Michael Ochs Archives/Stringer/Getty; p.173 Hulton Deutsch/Getty; p.174 Derzsi Elekes Andor, from Wikimedia Commons; pp.176–7 Walt Disney Co./Courtesy: Everett Collection/Alamy; pp.182–3 AKG-images/Niklaus Stauss; pp.186–7 Laurie Lewis/Bridgeman Images; p.188 *Mon Élue Noire* by Olivier Dubois – Photo: F. Stemmer.

Index

riots 13

Rite of Spring, The: Augurs of Spring 80–1, 135, 138, 141, 145, 148, 179; centenary celebrations 181; completion 84; complexity 85; composition 27, 73, 76–7, *78-9*, 80–1, 82; Dance of the Earth 117, 151–2; Dances of the Young Girls 145, 148, 149; deadline 77, 83; Debussy on 83–4; development 69–73, 76–7, 80–2; Diaghilev on 162; early work on 67–8; Evocation of the Ancestors 155; Glorification of the Chosen One 154–5; human sacrifice 71, 72; influence 165–8, 169, 171–4; inspiration 64–7; Introduction, Part 1 103, 107, 137, 144–5, 179; Introduction, Part 2 152–3; listening guide 144–59; and the modern world 13–4; Mystic Circles of the Young Girls 153–4; opening dance 107–8, 114; orchestra 89, 138–41; Part 1 71–2, 103, 127, 130, 144–5, 148–52; Part 2 72, 103, 127, 130, 152–6, 158–9; performances 122–3, 162–3, 165; playthrough 81, 82–3; post-Ballets Russes versions 188–91; Procession of the Sage 114; publication agreement 73; Puccini on 101–2; recordings 162; rehearsals 84, 86–9, 99; reviews 54; as ritual 67; Ritual Action of the Ancestors 155–6; Ritual of Abduction 148–9, 150; Ritual of the Rival Tribes 149, 150–1, 180; Roerich's guidance 76; roots 46–7; and Russian culture 35; Sacrificial Dance (The Chosen One) 115, 118–9, 138, 140, 156, 158–9, 184, 185; sacrificial victim 88; The Sage 151; scenario 12, 47, 70–1, 71–2, 80, 127, 130; seeds of innovations 60; sketches 80–1, 84; source 40; Spring Rounds 149–50, 156, 179; staging 82–3, 84–5; status 14–5; Stravinsky on 76, 162, 163, 190; Stravinsky's defence of 121–2; Stravinsky's instructions 165; Stravinsky's speed of work 82; structure 71, 76; title 72; as total work of art 12; as tragedy 190–1; transitions 131; working title 67; *see also* choreography; music; premiere; reviews

Rivière, Jacques 54, 115, 122, 178, 188, 190–1

rock music 172–4

Roerich, Nicholas 12, 46–7, 64–7, 76, 82, 84, 99, *104–5*, *106*, 107, *109*; *The Forefathers 146–7*; *The Idols* 66; 'Joy in Art' 66, 70; scenario 70–1, 80, 127; at Talashkino 69–73

Royal Ballet 185

Russia: artistic renewal 28, 30–7, 40, 42–3, 46–7

Russolo, Luigi 13